FUTURE
CHOICE

WHY NETWORK MARKETING
MAY BE YOUR
BEST CAREER MOVE

FUTURE CHOICE

WHY NETWORK MARKETING MAY BE YOUR BEST CAREER MOVE

MICHAEL S. CLOUSE

Nexera™ LLC Publishers *Lynnwood, Washington U.S.A.*

FUTURE CHOICE
WHY NETWORK MARKETING
MAY BE YOUR BEST CAREER MOVE

© 2006 by Michael S. Clouse

International Standard Book Number: 978-0-9635949-2-1
0-9635949-2-3

Nexera™ LLC
18423 – 12th Avenue West
Lynnwood, WA 98037-4900 U.S.A.

info@nexera.com
www.nexera.com/fc

U.S.A. 1 888 639 3722 International +1 425 774 4264

REVISED PRINTING

10 9 8 7 6

Table of Contents

Introduction
Scott DeGarmo, Editor-in-Chief
& Publisher, *SUCCESS* magazine..........................7

Preface 11

Chapter 1   2016, A Story 13

Chapter 2   A Business of Your Own 23

Chapter 3   One Plus One 33

Chapter 4   Profits and Prosperity 47

Chapter 5   Scoundrels and Visionaries.................57

Chapter 6   Your Graduate Education 67

Chapter 7   Challenges and Choices 91

Chapter 8   Success Does Leave Clues 99

Chapter 9   A Beginning.......................................113

Postscript 119

Appendix A Overcome the No-Time Syndrome....121

Appendix B Ethics 123

Biography 127

INTRODUCTION

I HEARTILY RECOMMEND THIS APTLY TITLED and well-written book to anyone seeking to learn about opportunities in Network Marketing.

I personally learned about the power of Network Marketing somewhat reluctantly. Like so many people, my mind was mainly closed on the subject. Then one of my editors at *SUCCESS* magazine began urging me to let him do a report for our readers on the topic. I explained to the staffer that, based on what little I knew, I had a hard time believing that Network Marketing could be seen as a serious way of building a business or making a living. "Some of the stories are simply too good to be true," I said, attempting to close the matter.

As it happened, I was dealing with Senior Editor Richard Poe, who had spent months examining the issue and preparing arguments to present to me and my other editors. In our ensuing editorial meetings, as Poe recounted statistics, case studies and anecdotes, I found myself becoming more receptive to his proposal.

However, some staffers considered the entire subject one to be shunned. As the opposing editors sensed my interest in the topic growing, they called a "time out" so they could gather material to present the opposite point of view. With the help of our researchers and our Nexus on-line service, our offices were soon flooded with Network Marketing articles from the national press. I read stacks of them, noting how public officials and regulators frequently made critical comments about Network Marketing or multi-level marketing, as it is often called.

But what all the previous coverage demonstrated to me was different from what my staff critics had intended. What the articles made clear was that the other side of the story—the positive side—had never been told. Why was this the case? Because the press in general, and the business press in particular, is, by and large, not opportunity-oriented. The journalistic mindset is inclined to be skeptical, critical, doubting, analytical—all important traits, to be sure. But what was needed to see the Network Marketing story was a receptive, entrepreneurial, future-oriented perspective—a mindset that seeks out what is good in an idea. Moreover, I concluded, the positive story was going to be a far more important one in the long run.

The article that was eventually published in *SUCCESS* magazine was the first fundamentally positive treatment of Network Marketing to appear in a major national publication. We pointed out how Network Marketing has often been wrongly confused with illegal pyramid schemes that convince people they can make money without working. We interviewed a range of experts, including Dr. Srikimar Rao, chairman of the marketing department at Long Island University and a student of MLM companies for nearly two decades. Dr. Rao began studying the field because he was aware that it had been ignored by mainstream researchers. Rao was one of the first academics to realize the enormous power of Network Marketing to create wealth. Our article also demonstrated how Network Marketing was being fueled by a pervasive sense of insecurity, an observation that seems more timely than ever today as we continue to witness tens of thousands of workers losing their jobs. Happily, many of these workers will find financial reward and personal freedom in Network Marketing.

Our conclusion was that Network Marketing is a powerful method of doing business that would grow in importance in the coming decade. The response to our coverage was so overwhelming that we have since made Network Marketing an ongoing part of our editorial coverage. Before the publication of *Future Choice*, no book for the general public had appeared on the subject. So, the publication of *Future Choice* was indeed a significant event.

Scott DeGarmo
Editor-in-Chief & Publisher
SUCCESS magazine

PREFACE

I N HIS BOOK, *All I Really Need to Know I Learned in Kindergarten*, author-philosopher Robert Fulghum tells the story of when Halley's Comet swept across our skies in 1910:

"The world was divided between those who celebrated and those who watched in fear and trembling," Fulghum wrote. Those who understood that the nighttime spectacle was a comet watched its fiery approach with awe and anticipation. Those who didn't watched in fear and dread. All experienced the same comet, but in radically different ways.

You always have the opportunity to live your life in those same two ways: in knowledgeable anticipation or in ignorance and fear.

It is a choice that shapes your future.

It is your *Future Choice.*

My goal in *Future Choice* is to introduce you to one unique opportunity for your life and work—Network Marketing. As you consider whether Network Marketing may be your best career move, I hope I can in some small way help you to be one of those men and women who choose their futures with knowledgeable anticipation.

1.

2016, A Story

"Over the next ten years we are poised
to create an additional 10 million millionaires."
—Paul Zane Pilzer
World-Renowned Economist,
New York Times Best-Selling Author

*S*usan Edison leaned against the doorway as she
looked across the deck of her Colorado home to the
wildflower-filled meadows and majestic mountains
beyond.

She sighed with contentment, then turned back
into the house reaching for her coffee cup as she moved
through the bright sunny kitchen, down the hall, and into
the living room.

Speaking commands to her digital home theater,
Susan instantly logged onto The Hologram Network and
selected a style of sofa she'd been thinking of buying. Immediately, the form of the couch appeared in the room,

in just the fabric she had requested.

Susan studied the three-dimensional sofa for a minute, then shook her head a little as she adjusted the theater's wireless touch pad to position the seemingly solid hologram closer to the fireplace. Within moments the video-capture unit automatically altered the sofa's fabric to one that more closely reflected the shades of the spring flowers outside.

Susan smiled. Yes, that was just right.

She pointed the remote back to the screen, clicked once, ordering the sofa and clicked again to request express home delivery. Satisfied, she spoke a command to turn off the plasma display.

Although the sofa disappeared, Susan knew it would be there in her living room in just one week.

Susan smiled again, thinking of Jennifer Wellington, her dentist, who would receive a commission on the purchase of the sofa.

By buying her sofa through The Hologram Network, Susan saved time, money, and was able to order exactly what she wanted—something the few remaining retail furniture stores rarely offered. Besides, shopping this way also allowed her to support Jennifer, who in addition to her dental practice, represented a company that offered a complete line of home furnishings, and in return was one of her own best customers.

Susan cast one last glance around her living room, pleased with the decision she'd made that morning, then walked upstairs to her spacious, in-home, corner office.

Only 10 minutes remained until her first appointment of the day…

Later that morning Susan held a private international conference call with thirty of her top business associates. She then addressed 1,500 new prospects through her wireless hologram network, streamed live each Tuesday morning via her personal Web Portal. And with a single push of a button, she sent her weekly e-mail newsletter to 137,000 of her own consultants around the world.

After lunch on her deck, Susan strolled down to the lake. The children would be home soon. This was her best chance for a few minutes to herself after a busy morning.

She'd come a long way in the last ten years, since 2006 when she first began her own home-based business. And all because she'd listened to a friend, tried a few products, and then accepted the invitation to become an Independent Consultant herself.

Again, Susan smiled.

It may be the wave of the future. No boss, set your own hours, succeed or fail by your own efforts, all with a computer, high-speed Internet connection, and a mobile phone—preferably from the sunny deck of your new custom-built home...

According to a survey commissioned by *Yahoo!*, 72 percent of adults have considered starting their own businesses. Today, more than 34.9 million people work at home, full- or part-time, as self-employed business entrepreneurs or telecommuters. Millions of people design boats, make wine, create manuscripts or broker information from a re-designed corner in the garage or a spare room in the house.

Hewlett-Packard, Apple Computer, Mrs. Fields' Cookies, Domino's Pizza, Nike, and Walt Disney Productions all started as home-based businesses. Therefore, whether your dream is to catapult your own company into the Fortune 500 or to blend home life and work life into one seamless existence, business forecasters say today's updated version of home-based entrepreneurship may be the best model for the businesses of the future.

Patricia Aburdene and John Naisbitt write in their book, *Megatrends for Women*, "There are two ways to the CEO's chair. The corporate route: Draw up a five- or ten-year plan to gather the skills for the top-executive job you hope to land... And the entrepreneurial approach: Start your own business now."

It appears many are choosing to chart their own course.

According to the Department of Labor statistics over 1,500 new home-based businesses are opened every day. And these businesses enjoy a healthy rate of success. According to the Home-Based Business Institute about 70% of home-based businesses will last over a three-year period, compared to 29% of other business ventures. But what is causing this interest in self-employment?

Self-employment hit its low point in the 1980s, at 8.6 million. That number climbed to 10.5 million by 1994, and by 2003 the number of self-employed in the U.S. increased to 18.6 million people. And the numbers continue to rise...

Several business trends are converging to spur this return to self-employment. One is the economy itself.

As we continue evolving from an industrial society to one based on information and services, the way we earn our living is changing as well. Yet for too many of us, the change has been a painful one.

Fortune 500 companies shed 9 million jobs during the past decade. General Motors, IBM, and AT&T, corporations once considered a ticket to lifelong employment security, are jettisoning middle-management layers—and the employees that go with them—by the tens of thousands.

In an effort to find a place in the evolving global economy, companies are selling off or closing down plants or entire divisions. They are centralizing and economizing, outsourcing and contracting. Entire industries are moving overseas and taking with them the security of those who once depended on them for their life's work.

As corporations continue to consolidate operations, labor analysts say the number of corporate-based jobs will continue to decline. "The bond of loyalty between employer and employee has been broken by the merger mania and the 'lean and mean' response to global competition," writes Gerald Celente, a New York-based trends analyst in his book, *Trend Tracking*.

"If you work for a corporation, you can no longer sit back and enjoy the comfort of job security. If you're a top executive, you may have a golden parachute that will give you a nice soft landing. But if you're a senior executive, a middle manager or just an employee, you have nothing to protect you other than your ability to get a job somewhere else."

But where else?

And at what salary?

Indeed, many of yesterday's higher-paying manufacturing jobs now live overseas and still others are packing their bags for the trip abroad...

The number of U.S. owned plants in Mexico alone have increased steadily, from 1,700 in 1990, to more than 3,800 plants today. And the National Institute of Statistics, Geography and Information in Mexico, reports the number of workers in foreign-owned (chiefly US-owned) plants almost doubled in the past decade, from 648,000 workers in 1995 to 1,167,000 workers in 2005.

Those numbers are expected to climb...

And while their public relations officers say they regret the impact on U.S. workers, companies as diverse as Zenith and Fisher-Price say if they want to remain competitive they have no choice but to move to countries where wage rates are lower.

For the first time in our economic history, the cutbacks are slicing as deep into executive suites as they have into blue-collar production lines. Bank presidents, stock analysts, and entire corporate public relations departments are now just as likely as a GM auto worker to find themselves suddenly unemployed.

Whatever the job classification, the contraction is not confined to marginal employees with limited skills. Today's unemployment lines are full of bright, motivated and engaging people—people who have much to offer. Unfortunately, the loss of their jobs is not temporary, nor is it part of a typical, short-term business cycle—because most of the jobs lost in the last decade will not return.

North Americans have come to rely on a three-legged financial stool to provide them with economic security: A private pension, Social Security and their personal savings. But for both men and women, that formula has all but disappeared.

Personal debt is at an all-time high, and the U.S. national savings rate remains among the lowest in the industrialized world. As a result *Money* magazine now publishes advice on *What to Do with $5,000* because it appears that's all many readers have to invest. Even workers who hope to receive a full pension at retirement are not assured a comfortable life... It's sad, but true: Social Security Administration statistics show the median private pension for married men is $8,400 a year, or less than $162 a week; for married women it is $4,365 a year, or just $84 a week.

Really, the question isn't whether average pension rates are too low, but whether those counting on a pension will actually receive one at all...

According to NBC Evening News Anchor Brian Williams, "For a few years now Baby Boomers have heard, and consistently ignored, the warnings: Not to count on your pension or Social Security when you retire. So now millions of Americans are scrambling to finds ways to make sure their Golden Years are indeed golden."

As the reality begins to sink in, many Americans are beginning to wonder if their pensions will survive, or if their pensions will simply become a broken promise they've worked for all their lives.

And just because a company is healthy doesn't mean your pension is guaranteed. Increasingly, well-known companies are pulling the plug on pensions. According to one study, 26 Fortune 1000 companies pulled the plug in 2004, nearly a 58% jump over 2003. CNBC News Correspondent Scott Cohn reported, "Companies complain the plans are too expensive and too complex. Whatever the reason, across America a decades-old bond between employer and employee is now strained to the breaking point."

It seems the traditional three-legged stool of financial security has developed a marked wobble...

That financial wobble is one reason millions of North Americans are choosing to embrace a newly designed economic stool—one with four solid legs on the ground.

That fourth leg is ownership of their own full- or part-time home-based business.

And today record numbers of us *are* choosing to chart our own economic future, to live by our own business wits.

By the end of 2005, 32 percent of all U.S. households had an income-producing or after-hours home office, generating an average income of $63,000 a year. Some of those new business owners want to build an empire; others want only to make a second income, one that will provide the difference between living and living well.

Indeed, financial experts say the quality of life for millions of North Americans would increase significantly if they were able to increase their income by only $500 a month! That's enough to start an investment account or to buy a more reliable car. And it's more than enough to begin golf lessons, take the family to Disneyland, or pay off a credit card.

All that and more, is possible. Because between today's economic uncertainty and the idyllic lifestyle of our futuristic friend—21st century entrepreneur Susan Edison—lies one of the business world's best kept secrets, and certainly one of its most profound and potent opportunities.

Michael S. Clouse

2.

A Business of Your Own

"The richest people in the world build networks.
Everyone else is trained to look for work."
—Robert T. Kiyosaki
Author, *Rich Dad Poor Dad*

IN 1987, DONNA JOHNSON was a 29 year old mother of three who coached the girls swim team for Appleton East High School... Today, she earns almost ten times more than the President of the United States. In addition to the lakefront summer home in northern Wisconsin, her income just bought her family a sprawling new winter estate in the Southwest. And Donna's husband Gary, was able to retire at age 50 to spend more time with their family.

Donna used her belief in the company, consistent activity, and stick-to-itiveness to turn a hot idea into a career, the classic recipe of a successful entrepreneur.

Donna Johnson is one of the top Independent Executive National Vice Presidents for a California-based company that distributes over 300 pure safe and beneficial anti-aging and wellness products to customers throughout North America. Since 1980 Arbonne International—one of the largest direct-marketing companies in the world—has used independent consultants to sell its products. Donna now works through an international organization of consultants that she, or someone in her Network, introduced to the company.

Donna is paid a commission on all her retail sales and a bonus on purchases made within her Network organization. Because she chose a company right for her, committed to their system, and stayed the course, she earns more money than most top CEOs.

"Before I became involved, I basically thought Network Marketing wasn't a real business," says Kathy Lutz of Bel Air, Maryland, who in 1999 started her own home-based business. "But when I tried the products I was amazed at the benefits! It was then that I began to realize if others felt the same way I did, this could work. In May of 1999 I left my position with upper management in one of the largest banking corporations in Maryland. Three years later I was earning more than twice my corporate salary working one-third of the hours!"

Growing numbers of people like Kathy Lutz and Donna Johnson are looking at the other side of today's global economic uncertainty—the opportunity side. Their home-based businesses allow them to understand and take advantage of today's business trends—not to fear them. They're building long-term residual income and personal freedom using a business concept known today as Network Marketing.

Network Marketing, sometimes called Multi-Level Marketing or MLM, is one of several ways to move products from manufacturers to consumers. Although Network Marketing is not a new concept, more often than not it is still misunderstood.

Network Marketing is simply an alternative distribution system to those used by most major corporations today. While other more common forms of distribution are under stress—witness the rash of bankruptcies in the wholesale/retail industry—Network Marketing is expanding rapidly.

To illustrate why, let's take a look at some of the methods companies have developed to move their products from the manufacturer to the consumer. The most well known of course, is the retail channel...

Corporations spend enormous amounts of money, sometimes as much as $10 or $20 million per advertising campaign, to make you want to buy what they have to sell. Advertising may make you laugh, or it may make you grit your teeth, but if it gets you to buy what the company is selling, it's a success.

Yet the cost of all that advertising is just the beginning. Long before you've even warmed up your car, or before your children have begged you into promising them the latest TV-inspired fad, those companies have sold their products—at a profit, of course—to wholesalers across the country.

Wholesalers sell those same products to distributors who in turn pay another entire layer of middlemen—truckers, warehouse workers, clerical employees, etc., and add their costs and their profits to the prices of the items you want to buy.

Next, your increasingly more expensive product moves into the retail store where, in many industries, distributors must pay an additional "slotting" fee to win the product a space on a retail shelf. That fee, like all the others, gets passed on to you, as does the cost of the store's advertising, its light bill, the cost of its employees' health insurance, vacations, and "shrinkage"—another word for what gets broken or stolen.

It shouldn't surprise *you*—the shopper those advertisers spent millions of dollars to attract—to hear an almost audible sigh of relief across the retail landscape when you pull into a mall parking lot.

Yet you may not.

You may be too busy searching for a parking place or negotiating through a maze of store corridors specifically designed to confuse you. And if you do find your item of interest, you will then wait in line to pay for it, balancing your purchase in one hand while you attempt to reach for your two forms of identification with the other...

There must be a better way, and consumers are constantly searching for it.

Each week millions of people travel to large discount warehouse stores where buying clubs offer rock-bottom prices on mass merchandise to qualified members in exchange for a small annual fee. These shoppers choose to trade service, convenience, and "limited time only" availability for, hopefully, the best price.

Others find they prefer shopping online. Indeed, companies such as Amazon.com, Buy.com, and Overstock.com offer today's consumer almost anything imaginable.

Some specialty companies, such as L.L.Bean, have refined the art of shopping—first by catalog and now online—even further and market it as a more pleasant alternative to retail shopping.

A number of such online, or mail-order companies, have developed followings of loyal customers who look forward to receiving each e-mail announcement and/or new catalog. Their products often are of a quality and selection unavailable in most retail stores, and goods are shipped to buyers' homes, with 100 percent satisfaction guaranteed.

Network Marketing seeks to combine the best aspects of all these distribution systems: the high quality merchandise offered by the best specialty stores, the convenience of online or catalog shopping, the cost savings of buying direct, and the time-saving value of to-your-door delivery. Then it takes the concept one step further. Network Marketing pays you to participate in its form of sales and distribution.

SUCCESS magazine called Network Marketing "the most powerful way to reach consumers…" In fact, dozens of the most innovative companies are taking a closer look at Network Marketing, because, as a delivery method of goods and services, it complements the world's developing business trends.

"Manufacturers are looking for a way to spend advertising dollars as close to the point of sale as possible," writes business author Charles Whitlock in his book, *How To Get Rich.*

"That's what Network Marketing does: it provides a one-on-one presentation to potential customers right at the point of sale. A person who wants to buy doesn't have to turn off the TV and go to the market, dial an 800 number or mail anything in. All the customer has to do is say, 'Yes.' And the customer is likely to say, 'Yes,' because MLM distributors are usually among the most enthusiastic and committed sales professionals in the marketplace."

Today a consumer can buy almost anything through Network Marketing, from anti-aging skincare and wellness products, to identity theft insurance, to kitchen cutlery. And a number of the nation's most successful corporations have built their business exclusively through Network Marketing. Other Fortune 500 companies have complete Network Marketing subsidiaries, including Colgate-Palmolive and Gillette. Jockey International and the Body Shop, for example, have rolled out in-home direct-selling units, with products that are sometimes identical to those offered in stores. Southern Living magazine introduced *Southern Living at Home*, where shoppers can buy products seen in the magazine. Other companies are creating partnerships with Network Marketing companies as well...

When MCI turned to Amway to market their long distance service through their network of independent business owners, the joint venture worked. *Three million subscribers later*, AT&T, stung by the potency of Network Marketing, launched its now infamous "We want you back" advertising campaign.

Some of the highest quality and most innovative products over the years have been marketed solely through independent distributors. Sewing machines, smoke detectors and vacuum cleaners all were first introduced into the marketplace through direct selling channels.

Business analysts predict the amount of goods and services that move through these direct selling channels will increase at a rate of 30 percent per year in the next few years, many times the rate of growth predicted for the economy as a whole. Part of the reason is that the products most commonly marketed today through Network Marketing are those that will be appealing to the baby boomer generation as they move through middle age.

Trend trackers say baby boomers are searching for youthful appearance, fitness, and convenience. They crave products that will make them healthy and attractive; *and* they're willing to pay for what they want, even in lean times, because they feel they deserve it.

Internationally known futurist Faith Popcorn calls this trend "egonomics."

"It's about individuating, differentiating, customizing," she writes in her bestseller, *The Popcorn Report*. "And it's a major force to reckon with in today's marketplace. Egonomics means simply this: there is profit to be reaped in providing for the consumer's need for personalization, whether it be in product concept, product design, or personal service."

Network Marketing companies have been on the forefront of those trends for years with all-natural food supplements, pure safe and beneficial skincare products, and earth-friendly recyclable packaging. As this massive group of consumers moves into the most vibrant and active middle years yet known, Network Marketing companies await them with products to help fight wrinkles, lose excess weight, and protect the quality of their lives.

Additionally, according to Popcorn's research, people are also "retrenching."

They see the frenzy in their lives and they are looking for ways to create a more serene and prosperous future for themselves and those they love. They are searching for ways to build that future without sacrificing themselves and their values in the process.

It's a movement authors Patricia Aburdene and John Naisbitt call "the search for opportunity, leadership, and balance." It is a search for ways to work smarter, live smarter, and make smarter choices, so there is more left to give to families, friends, and to ourselves. It is a desire to create something of value and integrity with which to shape a future of joy and prosperity.

For millions of people, that's just the opportunity Network Marketing offers.

3.

ONE PLUS ONE

"If you don't run your own life,
somebody else will."
—John Atkinson (1884 - 1932)

IN 1990, SANDRA TILLINGHAST was living the new American dream. She had made the leap small business advocates Paul and Sarah Edwards had predicted, to a home-based business of her own.

As a somewhat successful entrepreneur, Sandra was already doing what she thought she loved when a friend introduced her to a product that literally changed her life. "I couldn't believe how much I liked the product," Sandra recalls, "Then I looked at the opportunity and my instinct told me making a move was the right thing to do."

But giving up what you've got in order to get what

you want is not always easy. "As a single parent, leaving a business where I was already making $5,000 a month and enjoying the added benefit of a company car was a risk. To get through the transition I put a sticker on my calendar, with a quote from Helen Keller, and read it out loud every day: 'Life is either a daring journey or it is nothing at all.'"

The words David McNally wrote in his book, *Even Eagles Need A Push*, also helped. "The eagle gently coaxed her offspring toward the edge of the nest. Her heart quivered with conflicting emotions as she felt their resistance to her persistent nudging. Why does the thrill of soaring have to begin with the fear of falling? The eagle drew courage from an innate wisdom. Until her children discovered their wings, there was no purpose for their lives. Until they learned how to soar, they would fail to understand the privilege it was to have been born an eagle. And, so one by one she pushed them...and they flew!"

"I wasn't always the eagle." Sandra recalls. "Sometimes I felt like a chicken." She offers this advice. "If your intention is to build a successful home-based business that would allow you time *and* financial freedom, at some point you will need to take the first step—even if that first step appears difficult. In other words, make the decision, get started, and then give it everything you've got."

In the beginning, "No" was a hard word for Sandra to hear, but she learned how to move on, or go back and try again to turn that "No" into a "Yes!" She also learned how not to take rejection personally. "My job is to try and make a difference wherever I can by sharing the opportunity and products with those I continue to meet."

Today, Sandra, along with her husband Ted, is living an extraordinary life. "My seven-figure annual income, along with the free time to enjoy it, allowed us to build our dream home at the beach in Southern California. Today, I am so grateful I listened to my inner voice. True, it took an ongoing commitment, consistent effort, and belief in the fact that I could do this... I guess you could say, I took care of my business and it took care of me."

The Tillinghasts are not alone in their move into Network Marketing. The Direct Selling Association, one of several industry associations, estimates sales of goods and services sold in the U.S. by Network Marketing and Direct Sales companies reached $30 billion, while the World-Wide Federation of Direct Selling Associations (WFDSA) reported international sales (including the U.S.) of $96.93 billion.

The WFDSA goes on to report that 57,417,853 people in more than 43 reporting countries were estimated to have earned an income from Network Marketing and Direct Sales, and those numbers continue to grow at the rate of 175,000 new distributors per week!

And that's not all... The recently released Ernst & Young Impact Study estimated the total economic effect on the U.S. economy to have reached $72 billion! That jaw-dropping figure included the direct and indirect compensation earned by the more than 13.6 million Americans who work in the Network Marketing and Direct Sales industry.

"I used to think the only way to have the lifestyle I really wanted was to find a profession I *somewhat* enjoyed and then climb the corporate ladder. But now I know the truth," says Janet Elliott, owner of her own Networking business. "My mid-six-figure annual income, along with the free time to enjoy with my husband, Bryan, and our three children, are living proof that in Network Marketing, you really can have it all."

The first experience many have with Network Marketing is when they are approached by someone they know to sample or try products from the company that person represents. In fact, ever since Alfred C. Fuller originated the door-to-door method of direct selling in 1906, tens of millions of people have purchased products or services from a Network entrepreneur. Even if they make purchases at first primarily to show support for a friend's new business venture, they often later find themselves returning when they discover the quality and value of those products and services.

Today there are four common ways to participate in Network Marketing:

AS A RETAIL CUSTOMER
Retail customers purchase products directly from

the person who introduced them to the company. In exchange for "paying a little more than wholesale" they receive personalized service.

AS A WHOLESALE BUYER

Most of those involved in Network Marketing sign up as a wholesale buyer with a company simply for the benefit of buying its products at wholesale. Wholesale buyers typically pay a nominal annual fee—much like those charged by membership-only discount stores—to buy their products at a reduced price directly from the company itself.

AS A PART-TIME NETWORKER

Like wholesale buyers, part-time Networkers buy and use their companies' products for themselves and their families. Additionally, they also share information about their favorite products with their friends, neighbors, and business associates. When they help others sign up to obtain the same products and discounts they receive, they qualify to earn income based on the sales volume generated.

Although many professional Networkers like Donna Johnson and Kathy Lutz who we met earlier go on to earn large monthly bonuses, they typically begin as wholesale buyers or as part-time business-builders. Indeed, the Direct Selling Association estimates that at any given time, almost 90 percent of all Networkers work their business part-time.

Experienced Networkers tell us that people who consistently work their businesses part-time can expect to earn incomes from $500 to $5,000 a month or more as their Networks grow. Those who build sizeable Network organizations, or who sponsor others who do so, can earn incomes many times beyond that...

As you read these words, tens of thousands of part-time Networking professionals are matching—sometimes many times over—the salaries they earn at their full-time jobs. It's true. People begin a Network Marketing business with the idea of making an extra $500 or even $1,000 per month. Then one day they realize that if they get serious about their business, they could make $3,000 or $5,000, or $7,000 per month or more.

AS A FULL-TIME NETWORKER

Those who decide to build a full-time Network Marketing business buy and use their company's products for themselves and their families. In addition, they work full-time to tell others about their company, its products and the business opportunity it presents.

"When I was first introduced to my company, I was a camp director attending graduate school..." recounts Independent Executive National Vice President Donna Weiser. "But without any background in Network Marketing or Direct Sales, most of the people in my life thought I was crazy to give up an MBA degree to sell skincare! Then last year my income exceeded $500,000. I had time to enjoy my life! And most of those people started thinking I was pretty smart."

Network Marketing's advantage is its ability to compensate company representatives not only for their own efforts, but also for the efforts of those they bring into their Network organization, even into fourth, fifth and subsequent levels of participation. So where does all that money come from? Network Marketing companies use the money that traditional companies spend on advertising and distribution to pay commissions and bonuses to their representatives, to those who are promoting the products directly to the consumer.

It's called the "exponential success path." And it is open to any Network Marketer—wholesale, part-time, or full-time—sometimes with astounding results. As a matter of fact, Network Marketers across the country, and around the world, are earning $10,000, $50,000, $100,000 and more. Per month! From home.

Networkers use two favorite examples to explain Networking's exponential compensation system. The first is called the "doubling concept." Here's an example:

Take one penny and set it aside. The next day, and every day thereafter, double the number of pennies you set aside.

It's simple. On the second day, you will have two cents; on the third day, four cents. By the end of the first week, you will have 64 cents. Now fasten your financial seat belt...

By the end of the second week, you will have accumulated $81.92. By the end of the third week, more than $10,000 and by the end of the month, you will have saved well over $5 million and will be scrambling for storage space for all those pennies!

Turn the pennies into people earning income on product sales, and turn the 30 days into 30 weeks, or 30 months, and the economic power of Network Marketing begins to emerge.

Here's how the doubling concept might work in real life, using Network Marketing's second common example:

Suppose that after finding a company whose products you believe in, and then learning about the power of Network Marketing, you pay the nominal distributorship fee (usually under $50) to become an independent consultant, and also order a little inventory to personally use, and share with your friends...

In the first month, you tell your friends and family about your new venture and share the benefits your products provide: they are pure, safe, and beneficial; you are able to save money buying them at wholesale prices; and you make an immediate profit by offering the products at retail prices to those who want to buy directly from you.

Now suppose that, in addition, you find one person who would like to join you, someone who likes the products, who also recognizes the potential of Network

Marketing, and who wants to do what you are doing.

At the end of your first month, in addition to saving money by purchasing your products wholesale and making profits from your own retail sales, you would also be earning income on the orders of the person you sponsored into the organization.

That's the beginning of what Network Marketers call a "downline," or a "successline." You now have two people in the organization—yourself and your first sponsored colleague. One plus one makes two. Maybe. *(See Figure 1)*

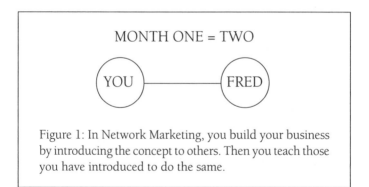

Figure 1: In Network Marketing, you build your business by introducing the concept to others. Then you teach those you have introduced to do the same.

To continue the example: What if in the second month you sponsored one additional person into the organization... And the person you sponsored also sponsors one person. Now you have four people in your organization and you're earning income on the sales volume generated by all four people, yet you yourself sponsored only two people. *(See Figure 2)*

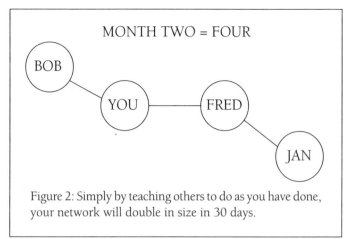

MONTH TWO = FOUR

Figure 2: Simply by teaching others to do as you have done, your network will double in size in 30 days.

In the *third* month of your business, you again sponsor one person—and so do each of those already in your group. Now you've grown to eight: you, the three people you have sponsored directly and the four others they have introduced to your business. *(See Figure 3)* Remember, this all could be happening before most other start-up businesses have earned a single penny of profit.

To show the true power of Network Marketing, let's follow a more "real-world" example.

Suppose you, as a part-time Network entrepreneur, decide to find two serious people who want to build a business as you are doing.

You sponsor two people, who sponsor two people, who sponsor two, who in turn sponsor two more. You would have 30 active people in your group, yet you

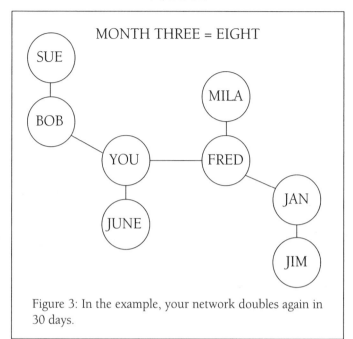

MONTH THREE = EIGHT

Figure 3: In the example, your network doubles again in 30 days.

yourself have sponsored only two people.

And what if you simply doubled your efforts? If you, as a serious business-builder, sponsored *four* people with similar ambitions, and then taught them to do the same, you would have a Network of 340 committed business-builders. If you sponsored five, and taught them to do the same, that number explodes to 780. Yet you personally sponsored only five people!

Now, here's where your efforts turn into income.

In Network Marketing, you receive compensation,

usually referred to as a bonus check, from the sales volume generated within your group. If each of your 780 people buys only $100 worth of products per month to use personally, to share as gifts, and to show to others, you and your group will have sold $78,000 worth of products. Depending on the compensation plan of your company, your bonus check could easily be $7,800 or more!

Even if each person in the organization buys only $50 worth of products or services each month, that still totals $39,000, which could bring you more than $3,900 a month. Remember, that's without any "sales superstars," any extra-achievers, or any large amount of retail sales. Just you and five of your colleagues teaching those you sponsor to build their organizations—as you have yours—each purchasing only $50 every month. (See *Figure 4*)

Figure 4. Look what would happen if you introduced five people into your business and taught each one to do the same. At the end of four months, you would have almost 800 people in your network.

		Total number in your group
You…		
teach five…	(5)	6
how to teach five…	(25)	31
to each sponsor five…	(125)	156
who will each sponsor five.	(625)	781

Similarly, Network Marketers across the country are using concepts just like these to build substantial incomes for themselves and their families, often part-time, from home. As we continue, let's look more closely at how they do this...

Michael S. Clouse

4.

PROFITS AND PROSPERITY

"The future is something which everyone reaches
at the rate of sixty minutes an hour,
whatever he does, whoever he is."
—C. S. Lewis, British author and scholar

I N 1990 MARTHA MCINTYRE WAS A STAY-AT-HOME MOM with two small children. Today, she is a Network Marketing phenomenon. Although she originally signed up to buy her products at a discount, Martha quickly realized selling those products to others would be a great way to earn an extra $200 per month. "In the beginning, I really didn't understand the concept of the 'business,'" Martha said. "And I really didn't want my family and friends to see me as one of those pushy Network Marketers."

Because of her initial lack of belief, Martha's journey took time... "Eighteen months passed before I was promoted to Area Manager" Martha said. "It was another eighteen months before I qualified to receive my white Mercedes-Benz cash bonus." Twenty-four months later—five years from the time she had originally signed up—Martha was promoted to Independent National Vice President.

However, along the way Martha began to change the way she felt about the "business" side of Network Marketing. "After I became an Area Manager, I started reading books about this business," Martha said. "What I discovered built my belief; this business was about duplication." After educating herself about Network Marketing, Martha realized she could better help others by sharing both the business opportunity *and* the products.

As the years passed, Martha continued learning, sharing, and growing her business.

Today Martha and her husband, Bret, are enjoying the finer things in life. Because of their Network Marketing business, Bret was able to retire at 45 years of age from his civil engineering position with the Oklahoma City highway department. Although diagnosed with Multiple Sclerosis in 1996, Martha is still able to be home with her three children, having the flexibility to choose when she works her business. "If you keep your priorities straight: God first, family second, and your career third, everything will fit into place," Martha said. Adding, "If you also remember that school is never out...

Because there are so many new things to learn."

By the way, according to her company's 2005 Independent Consultant Compensation Summary: Area Managers are paid an average of $1,551 per month; Independent Regional Vice Presidents are paid an average of $6,773 per month; and Independent National Vice Presidents are paid an average of $31,348 per month.

When asked about her own income, Martha simply smiled warmly and replied... "By sharing the products and opportunity with others, and successfully duplicating ourselves, we've been fortunate to earn an income above the published averages for our compensation plan."

How is that possible?

Leading Networkers across the country are making $10,000, $50,000, even $100,000 per month, by putting two concepts—exponential growth and indirect compensation—to work in their businesses...

As we saw earlier, all Network Marketing companies compensate their representatives through some form of exponential bonus payment. As a distributor, you receive commissions on your personal sales and bonuses on all purchases made in your group. Your income grows as the amount of product sold by members of your group grows. Therefore your compensation is directly linked to the combined efforts of the organization, *not* to some artificial outside evaluation of how much your skills and talents are worth, as is often the case with a traditional salary.

And there is no limit to how well your efforts can be rewarded. There are no salary freezes or caps, no waiting to see if your company will offer a production bonus. Office politics play no part in your compensation; neither does favoritism.

With indirect compensation, you once again profit not only from your own work, but from the work of a growing number of others as well. You're on the same team, and joint team goals build strong partnerships. *You* benefit from the work of your associates; *everyone* benefits from the effort you contribute...

As you learn your business, you also teach, coach, and inspire the other members of your team. They become more effective business owners in their own right, and all of you experience greater prosperity and higher levels of accomplishment. As their businesses grow, they do the same with their teams—they continue your legacy of success and you all continue to prosper.

Once you've established your Network, you can take an extended vacation, spend more time with your family, or decide to just swing in a hammock for a while and your business will continue to grow.

Terre Krotzer of Buckley, Washington, a leader of a rapidly growing group, recently took her entire family (five children plus two of their children's friends) to Disneyland for 10 days. They spent five days at the park, stayed at the best hotel, ate out every night, and were able to enjoy time together as a family. And the best part of the trip? Terre returned to discover that her company had been depositing override income into the Krotzer's bank account faster than the family had been spending it... That's when Terre realized, "Wow maybe we should go on vacation more often!"

The exact formula by which a Network Marketing company rewards its distributors is called a "compensation plan." Compensation plans vary from company to company. Each includes certain qualifications, or requirements, based on the company's products, its philosophy, the customer base it is trying to reach, and its vision of the future.

Most plans encourage consultants to build their organizations wide, that is, to sponsor many people personally. And they usually provide the greatest compensation, or income, to those who effectively teach their new people how to likewise sponsor others. With these plans, sponsoring wide creates wealth and building depth assures security—and you definitely want both.

Skeptics argue that compensation plans based on exponential growth are sure to implode under the weight of their own development. True, carried to its extreme, the concept of exponential growth would, at least on paper, have everyone in the world signed up as a distributor to some company in short order, leaving no one for those who enter late to sponsor.

But that's not going to happen. Although 175,000 people per week are joining a Network Marketing company somewhere in the world, not everyone wants to build a Networking *business*. They may just want to purchase products at wholesale, or the timing may not be right, and so on. Some will never be interested in building a business. Others will join a company only to drop out when they don't find a way to get rich quick, or find an immediate solution to whatever problems confront them.

Experienced Networkers say those who begin part-time, who take the time to learn their business, and who make a commitment to stick to it, can expect to earn from several hundred to several thousand dollars per month. The opportunity for full-time Networkers is unlimited—depending only on the time, energy, and the skill they bring to their work. Yet no matter what the compensation level, prosperity is more than a bonus check, and Networking offers additional, equally tangible rewards:

TAX ADVANTAGES

As owner of your own home-based business, you may be eligible for potent tax advantages and retirement savings. Check carefully with your accountant. Many of the costs of doing business are tax deductible, even if the people you're doing business with are family and friends.

SMALL INITIAL INVESTMENT

You can begin your business with a small initial

investment. Today, for example, franchises provide one of the most popular ways to be self-employed. But franchises can cost from $10,000 to $1 million and inventory and equipment can cost as much again or more.

Most franchise owners begin their new ventures under a load of debt. For their investment, they receive the right to use the name of a well-known company, along with company support and training in a proven method of operation. Those are the very same things you, as owner of your own Network Marketing business, will receive from your company and your sponsor, usually for less than $2,000.

LOW OVERHEAD

As a Network Marketer, you can begin your business immediately with virtually no overhead, no leases, no employees, no contracts, no accounts receivable and very little inventory. In fact, most companies are so sophisticated that all paperwork, even collection and distribution of sales tax, is handled directly by the company. You only assume responsibility for making sure your home-based business meets state and local regulations.

IMMEDIATE PROFITS

Business consultants say most small start-up businesses should be prepared to lose money for up to a year as they build their customer base. You, on the other hand, are poised for immediate success, because you can pay for your own growth out of business profits realized from day one!

FLEXIBLE HOURS

If you're already employed, you can begin your Networking business while retaining your present job. Again, almost 90 percent of Network Marketers work their businesses part-time, and many of today's industry leaders began building their empires by only investing 10 to 15 hours per week.

Because in Network Marketing, you are free to fit your work around your life, not your life around your work. You can arrange your business hours so you can be available for your children, your spouse, and your friends...and you can choose with whom you work, as well. You build your organization to include those who add enjoyment and satisfaction to your life—your customers are people you already care about, in addition to those you meet along your way to greater achievement.

Some people find they enjoy their new business so much they simply decide to grow it large enough to become their primary source of income. Others turn to their Network Marketing business when they lose their regular job. And some decide early on to commit to becoming a Network leader. Their dream is to build a significant income, one that allows them a higher level of financial security *and* time freedom.

All these business building strategies are possible...

The advantage of Network Marketing is that you decide how fast you want to grow your business. And you decide if and when to change that strategy.

FAMILY TIME

Your new business may even offer a chance to get to know your family better. "A moonlight business happens to be especially suited for family enterprises, because of the obvious built-in support and mutual assistance afforded by members of the family: a built-in, already functioning combination of interests," writes Philip Holland in *How to Start a Business Without Quitting Your Job.*

"The business will produce not only collective income, but also the opportunity to work in harmony for a common cause. Indeed, the economic interdependence of a family business can become the cohesive remedy for the splintered nature of contemporary family life."

Yet even with all the above tangible advantages, the most powerful reward may be the personal satisfaction that comes from within...

As a Network Marketing business owner, you are free to choose the speed at which you chart your course to success. You, with guidance and support from your sponsor and company, simply decide on the income you want to earn—and how fast you want to earn it—and then follow your company's proven business plan. Your time is your own. No boss looks over your shoulder; you punch no time clock.

"Playing the role of entrepreneur can provide a marvelous contrast from the frustrations inherent in salaried jobs," Holland writes. "It will offset the muddy compromises one must wade through when working for others. It will provide the opportunity for self-realization that eludes us at work. The exercise of final authority will revitalize your mental and physical powers and tap into a reservoir of strength unrealized during the absence of opportunity. Being president is exhilarating and can properly be described as the sweetest morsel in the candy store."

5.

SCOUNDRELS AND VISIONARIES

"A pessimist sees the difficulty in every opportunity; an
optimist sees the opportunity in every difficulty."
—Sir Winston Churchill

I F NETWORK MARKETING is such a powerful way to build
individual wealth, why aren't more of the world's
business leaders talking about it? And why is it you
are less likely to learn about this concept from a profes-
sor of economics, and more likely to hear about it from
your best friend's sister?

That's the magic of Network Marketing...

Remember, companies who choose to distribute
their goods and services through Network Marketers
don't spend millions of dollars on primetime advertisements, Sunday morning "infomercials" or on enough
direct mailers and magazine ads to doom several na-

tional forests.

Instead, Network Marketing relies on the oldest, most powerful advertising medium ever devised—word of mouth.

Mark tells a business colleague, Sue, about his new part-time venture. Sue becomes intrigued and tells Jan, her doctor. Jan, seeing the success Sue begins to enjoy, becomes involved and tells her brother and her stockbroker. At the end of just that one chain of conversational events, Mark finds himself working with four new business builders, receiving bonuses from all their sales and from all those who follow them. Mark's business grows from one simple conversation with a co-worker.

Just because Network Marketing is not yet taught at the Harvard Business School doesn't mean it isn't a powerful economic force with its own rich history.

"The concept of using a geometric progression to establish control within an organization, or to pass along information, has been present for centuries," writes Michael Harden, in his industry study, *The Handbook of Multi-Level Marketing.*

"Before the written word, primitive societies would pass legends, stories and other tribal information on to younger members of the tribe. They, in turn, would pass the information on to the next generation. Of course, as this process continued with each generation, new information and stories were added, thereby increasing each generation's knowledge."

Throughout the centuries Network Marketing, like all powerful concepts, has evolved. As with any economic system, it has been molded through the years by geniuses and scoundrels...by visionaries and the occasional huckster.

One of the first modern uses of the concept of exponential growth to generate income may have been the chain letter craze that swept the U.S. after World War I. The letters promised great profit if you would just send a dime—or sometimes a dollar—to the person at the top of the list and add your name to the bottom.

The chain letters spread as far as Europe and by the mid-1930s, the U.S. post office estimated that 10 million such letters were being mailed each day—even as postal authorities and law enforcement agencies battled the fraudulent schemes. The chain letter phenomenon began to subside in the early 1940s, although school children and an occasional adult may still receive a current version, usually without the unlawful request for money.

Modern Network Marketing is over 50 years old. More commonly known then as multi-level marketing, it began in the mid-1940s with the NutraLite Food Supplement Corporation. "Like many truly innovative breakthroughs," the development of true Network Marketing was an accident, writes David Stewart, in his book *Network Marketing: An Action Guide for Success*.

NutraLite, a company that offered food supplements,

originally was organized as a direct selling company. Independent distributors would buy its products and resell them directly to consumers. "NutraLite's products proved to be so popular and beneficial that the company found consumers were recommending them to their friends and becoming distributors based on their enjoyment of the product's benefits and a desire for additional income. That was a far cry from the cold-calling on strangers, hype and high-pressure techniques employed by door-to-door and conventional sales," Stewart writes.

In 1943, NutraLite restructured its marketing program to encourage each of its distributors to build—and be compensated for—their own individual sales organizations. Distributors were to receive bonuses on product sales made by those they sponsored, through a certain number of levels.

In 1956, NutraLite was joined by Dr. Forrest Shaklee, who founded the Shaklee company to gain wider distribution of the food supplements he had developed in his clinic. Over the years, Shaklee has grown to include more than 700,000 distributors—who have collectively earned over three billion dollars in commissions—by offering nutrition, personal care, and household products to the ultimate end-consumer.

Not long after, in 1959, former NutraLite distributors Rich DeVos and Jay Van Andel drew on the words "American" and "way" to name their own new personal and household products company Amway. Shaklee and

Amway, two of Network Marketing's true pioneers, paved the way for a new form of business.

As entrepreneurs rushed to adopt this new form of distribution, some overstepped the bounds of ethical business practices. Mutated forms of multi-level marketing turned into schemes designed to reward distributors solely for signing up other distributors, *not* for marketing legitimate products. Some companies forced distributors to pay huge up-front fees or hidden charges for questionable reasons, and then disappeared. These schemes came to be known as "illegal pyramids," because they often rewarded those first enticed into the organization, to the detriment of those who joined later.

In 1974, Senator Walter Mondale declared such companies to be the nation's number one consumer fraud. Companies such as Koscot Interplanetary, Holiday Magic and Bestline Products were shut down by government regulators.

Law enforcement agencies moved quickly to clean up the abuses. In the mid-1970s, burned by illegitimate schemes and scoundrels—and with still no clear idea of what constituted a legitimate use of multi-level marketing—the Federal Trade Commission and state agencies across the nation turned their wary eyes on almost all multi-level companies. In 1975, the FTC filed suit against Amway, alleging that the company was an illegal pyramid and that its refusal to sell its products in retail stores constituted a restraint of trade.

Amway spent four years and millions of dollars in

legal fees to defend its name. In 1979, the FTC ruled that Amway was not an illegal pyramid, that it did in fact generate substantial revenue from the sale of its products to consumers. In addition, the FTC acknowledged that Amway had "built a substantial manufacturing company and an efficient distribution system," according to Michael Harden's account of the settlement.

Amway and other multi-level companies that fought to prove their legitimacy won important victories for Network Marketing. And Network Marketing exploded in the next decade, as companies entered the newly vindicated industry...

"Every industry goes through an evolution," says Kelly Thayer, a former *Inc.* magazine Entrepreneur of the Year.

"In the 1960s as franchising was emerging, it was looked on as a scam, yet today more than 60 percent of all businesses are franchises," Thayer says. "Chiropractors were called the quacks of the 1970s. And look at the stock market; in the early days, the stock market was considered shady. All concepts run their course; they work the bugs out. In the coming decade you will see Network Marketing become an accepted way of marketing products."

The struggles in the early years of Network Marketing made important contributions to its future. They defined the ethics and standards by which the Network Marketing industry governs itself today. Government and industry officials continue to keep a close eye on questionable ventures that seem to search out the law's gray areas or look for loopholes in today's ethics and standards. That increase in credibility is one reason for Network Marketing's growth.

"Today we're seeing a change in the types of people attracted to this industry," says attorney Hugh Clemmons, Jr. "They demand more ethics and professionalism from the companies and they're refusing to do business with companies that don't live up to those expectations."

Network Marketing has evolved in other ways, as well...

Many of today's Network Marketing companies began as direct selling companies, in which independent distributors sold primarily to a large number of retail customers. Examples include Avon, Watkins, and The Fuller Brush Company. In the last few years, however, many direct selling companies have added Network Marketing divisions, or switched completely to Network Marketing.

Those who have made the move found they were still able to reach consumers because Network Marketers acquire their customers from people they know, or from people they meet as they go about their lives—known as "word-of-mouth advertising." They only sponsor those who are interested and then teach them to continue the process.

One other reason for the decline of direct selling is

that, beginning in the 1970s and continuing today, when distributors went door-to-door (Ding, Dong - Avon Calling!), no one was home. Women, long the customer backbone of direct sales, had entered the workforce in astounding numbers, leaving few behind to buy cosmetics, spices, and cleaning products.

Even companies like Tupperware whose business model focused exclusively on party plans, in which a "hostess" would gather a few of her friends for a presentation by an independent consultant, suffered. After a day at work, few women had the time or inclination to venture out again, even for what was usually billed as a social evening with friends.

Companies watching these societal trends moved quickly to revise their compensation plans to allow for other, more informal, methods of sales. According to the Direct Selling Association, more than 72 percent of sales are now conducted from one individual to another, one-to-one.

Although statistically 61.9 percent of sales are still transacted in the home, today they are more informal—friend to friend—rather than a traditional sales call, with 6.7 percent taking place in the workplace, and 3.96 percent taking place at a temporary location, like Starbucks.

Network Marketing has grown in the years since the 1979 Amway vindication, in both size and stature. Today's companies represent products and services that include those on the forefront of innovation and imagination, products that often are not available anywhere else. Network Marketers are leading the way with pure safe and beneficial products, products that today are helping us look younger, feel better, and truly live more rewarding lives.

Millions of independent men and women are representing their companies with integrity and grace. And they're reaping multiple rewards.

Michael S. Clouse

6.

YOUR GRADUATE EDUCATION

"The law of nature is
Do the thing, and you shall have the power..."
—Ralph Waldo Emerson

*S*usan Edison pushed herself back from the computer console in her office and laughed out loud—both at herself and at the vision of her friend Geoffrey on the screen in front of her.

Geoffrey grinned back at her.

"There's no way I'm going to make it to the Cape by Friday," he said. "My to-do list is leaning like the Tower of Pisa. I could be crushed at any moment. We'll be lucky if we make it by Sunday afternoon. How long are you staying? Theresa and I need to get back by the 15th. We're starting a new group in Stockholm and I promised to set up training sessions there by the end of the month."

"No problem," Susan said. "The kids and I are coming out on Tuesday, but Tom won't make it until the weekend. We're going to stay for a few weeks. As long as I have my computer, I can keep in touch as well there as here."

"Great," Geoffrey said. "We'll get a chance for a real visit. I'll get started on this list of ideas and e-mail you a progress report tomorrow.

"Hey, and give Andy a call, would you? He says Samantha has big news." With a wave, Geoffrey disappeared from the screen.

Susan laughed again. What a pair.

She never would have guessed Geoffrey and Andy would become such good friends. They were so very different...

Geoffrey was her banker when she had first started her business. He was a shrewd businessman, and he had watched the bank mergers and consolidations with a wary eye. When his community bank was bought out by a financial corporation in 2008, he took advantage of the bank's early retirement offer to its middle management. As he had brainstormed new career ideas, he remembered Susan's success and gave her a call to talk about the opportunities in Network Marketing.

Geoffrey had been a fast starter.

He used his ability to read people, his firsthand knowledge of their worries about financial insecurity and a high energy level to spread the word about his company's products and opportunities. Before the end of his second year in business, he had matched his former bank salary, and by the end of his third year, he had doubled it. Today, not only was his income enough to insure his family's future, he also had the free time to enjoy life together with them...

But Andy!

Andy had joined Susan about the same time as Geoffrey. He had been a young man with a good, steady job. When he talked with Susan he told her that he and his wife, Samantha, were looking for a second income, something that would allow them to provide their young children with a few of the extras in life. The trouble was, between their jobs, the children, and Andy's elderly parents, neither had much time to devote to any additional venture.

Even so, together with Susan they mapped out a few extra hours a week. Susan assured them that many people are able to build substantial part-time businesses in Network Marketing by committing only 10 to 15 hours a week. (See Appendix A)

Andy and Samantha took her at her word and went to work.

They told their friends, their family and their co-workers about their new business and introduced them to their company's products. When their friends and family found they could simply replace the products they were now using with ones of higher quality—and discovered they would be delivered directly to their door—some began to buy from Andy and Samantha at retail prices. That meant an immediate profit for their fledgling business.

Others, after trying some of the products, decided they wanted to buy them at wholesale prices directly from the company. That saved them money and earned Andy and Samantha a bonus every time someone placed an order.

One by one, over time, those they introduced to their company told others about the products and opportunities. As new people joined, Andy and Samantha's group grew. And so did their monthly bonus checks.

Neither of them quit their jobs. They didn't take out a loan to pay for business start-up costs. And they didn't have to leave their children in daycare to build their business. They simply told the people they knew—and those they met as they went about their day—about their company and its products. Some were interested enough to try the products. Others weren't. Some wanted to know more about the new business. Others never asked for more information.

Andy and Samantha didn't get rich quick. But by the time they had worked at their new business for a few months, they knew they were making progress toward their goals. They enjoyed sharing their discovery with those they knew. And although their bonus checks were small, they knew they were building the foundation for their family's future success.

Then something began to happen.

Samantha's Uncle Paul in Detroit bought one of the products. He introduced it to his buddies at work, who told their relatives, and suddenly Andy and Samantha had a hot group growing in Detroit. A couple of months later, Andy's sister's best friend in Dallas lost her job and decided to take her part-time Network Marketing business more seriously. By the end of the year, she was head of one of the fastest growing groups in the company and Andy and Samantha were shopping for tax shelters.

Now, eight years later, Geoffrey and Andy are golfing buddies with plans to start a snorkeling equipment company in the Cayman Islands, just for fun. They are two of Susan's top associates, yet each chose a different path to get them there.

Geoffrey started out fast and his success seemed to come just as rapidly.

Andy and Samantha—with help from Susan and their company—built their business at their own steady pace. They took time along the way to watch their children grow and to care for Andy's mother. Even so, only a few years later, their business provided them with much more than the extras they had first hoped for. It allowed them to build the life of their dreams. All by working a few consistent hours a week—with family, with friends, and with friends of friends....

No two Network Marketing companies are alike. Compensation plans differ, as do products and business philosophies. Each company has a different personality and a different focus. Some extremely reputable companies are flamboyant, others are more businesslike. Each approaches its product development, its distributor community, and its business decisions a little differently.

That aside, the best Network companies share several important characteristics. They adhere to the industry's highest principles and codes of ethics (*Appendix B*), they value their distributor community, and they constantly look for ways to improve both their products and their services.

If your best career move is to become a Network Marketing distributor, choosing the right company will be one of your most important decisions. Look for:

COMPANY EXPERIENCE IN NETWORK MARKETING

Other business experience is good, but you are looking for experience in Network Marketing. Network Marketing is an alternate method of product distribution. It also is a very different way to structure a company. Make sure the company you select has been in business long enough to prove it knows what it's doing. Many of the here-today, gone-tomorrow companies that fly through the Network Marketing community simply didn't know what they were getting into.

LENGTH OF TIME IN BUSINESS

There's a philosophy in Network Marketing that says if you get in on the ground floor of a hot new company, you'll rise to the top as it grows. Perhaps. But for every true opportunity, there are at least fifty companies that come on strong, then fizzle and fade, leaving their distributors confused, embarrassed, and without the income they have become accustomed to. You are much better off to catch the elevator on the third or fourth floor and ride the rest of the way to the top.

STRONG FINANCIAL BASE

More companies in all types of businesses fail because of lack of financial depth than all other reasons put together. Network Marketing companies, especially young ones, are under particular stress. They can grow rapidly, straining their ability to finance their growth responsibly. It takes a steady management hand on the wheel to chart a course between the rapid growth of Networking and a solid balance sheet for the future.

TOP COMPANY MANAGEMENT

You want that hand at the wheel to know which way it needs to steer. You want your company's management to be experienced, creative, and professional.

Check to see if the company you are considering is a member of an industry association such as the Direct Selling Association, or the World Federation of Direct Selling Associations. Those who join undergo close scrutiny and a membership waiting period, and they agree to adhere to the association's strict code of ethics.

COMPANY COMMITMENT TO ITS DISTRIBUTORS

The company you want to work for values its distributors. It is constantly looking for ways to improve its products, the way it does business, and its ability to help you do your job and build your business. It knows what you need and helps you in that regard.

Quality companies know their success depends on your success and they offer ongoing training, support, and encouragement. You need to know that your company is committed to your success and to its future as a Network Marketing business.

PROFESSIONAL-QUALITY PRESENTATION TOOLS

"I've found the business opportunity of a lifetime," a friend tells you. "You've *got* to take a look at this. Easy Street, here I come." Then she hands you a faded and crinkled photocopy of an outdated brochure. What are the chances you'll take her seriously?

Before you sign any enrollment agreement, make sure your company has the tools you will need to make your business a success. Tools like business cards and professional-looking and informative product catalogs and brochures. A full-color company presentation book, as well as a distributor training program are essential to your long-term success.

Once you know your company has them, order plenty of them. Nothing squelches a business presentation faster than finding yourself with someone who wants to know more about your company just as you remember you gave your last brochure to your brother-in-law.

PRODUCTS PEOPLE WILL WANT TO BUY

Your company's products don't need to be one-of-a-kind; giant Network Marketing companies have made billions of dollars by selling skincare and laundry detergent. Just make sure the Network company you choose offers products people want to buy because they are an exceptional value, they're of exceptional quality, or because they offer exceptional service and convenience. Whether it's skincare products, nutritional supplements, or identity theft protection, your customers must already use or really want what you have to offer.

EMPHASIS ON PRODUCTS

Legitimate Networking companies compensate their distributors for sales, not for sponsoring others. Their compensation plans are based on making sure the company's products get to the end consumers, whether retail or wholesale.

Although you will need products to use, share, and sell, legitimate companies do not require a large investment in inventory, known as front-loading. And they offer a liberal buy-back policy for any unsold inventory.

In addition, look for a company that offers your customers a money-back guarantee on products they purchase through you.

ROOM TO GROW

Do not automatically rule out a company who already has a strong market presence. Some very large and very successful companies already have tens of thousands of distributors, yet those who join still find success. There's no denying it may take more time and effort to build a large organization with a company that already has established a substantial presence in your area. But remember, in Network Marketing, you are building your business by introducing your products to those you know. Even if most of the world already uses your company's products, your friends and family may not, and you can still build a business by sharing your products and business success with them—and with those that they know...

DISTRIBUTOR SUPPORT

Networking is a simple business. Those at the top already know what works and what doesn't. There are keys to success in Networking, just as there are keys to success in any endeavor.

As a beginner, you may not know all those keys yet—and that's okay. Make sure your sponsorship team and the company you choose are committed to helping you learn them.

Strong support from your company's product knowledge department, marketing department, and sponsorship team can mean the difference between success and disappointment.

Indeed, strong support from your sponsor, as well as their sponsor and their sponsor's sponsor, are vital to reaching the level of achievement you have chosen. Before you join a company, ask how much help you can expect from those above you in the organization.

A PRODUCT YOU LOVE

In your career as a Networker, nothing will make your life simpler or more enjoyable than a catalog full of products or services you believe in. If you use and enjoy your company's products—and you must, for success—you will easily be able to recommend them to those you know.

Remember the last time you saw a movie you particularly enjoyed? Chances are the next day at work you recommended it to your co-workers. They may have gone to see the movie on your recommendation and taken a friend or spouse along with them. If they liked it, they may even have recommended it to others, who then also went to see the film. That's how movies turn into box office blockbusters!

Well, what if you received a check from the cinema for each person you or your friends referred? It would be a pleasant extra income, *and* you would have recommended the movie anyway, because you sincerely thought it provided a good evening's entertainment. Your company's products should play the same role.

Make sure you choose a company whose products you would use even if you did not market them or receive any compensation from their sale. Then your enthusiasm for them will spill over onto other's efforts and benefit everyone involved.

A SENSE OF FUN

One additional—and not entirely lighthearted piece

of advice: find a company that's fun. Find one that inspires you to greater heights of creativity, one that attracts positive people, the kind you'll look forward to spending time with. Many of the people in your company will become your closest associates and dearest friends. Make sure they add quality and integrity to your life, as well as income to your pocketbook.

As you begin your new business, you will need to be trained to ensure you have the greatest possible chance for success. We understand this in the business world... Imagine that tomorrow when you arrive at the office, your boss calls you in and presents you with an offer like this one:

"We like what you're doing here. We think you have a great future with this company. We see a period of strong growth ahead, so we've decided to invest in one of our most valuable assets—you.

"We'd like you to go back to school to get that advanced management degree you've talked about. We'll pay for the education. You can schedule your classes after work and on weekends. It probably will take you less than two years. When you've completed your work, we will immediately raise your salary by $5,000 a month. And you'll have an education that will benefit you for the rest of your career. All you need to do is invest some of your spare time. Are you interested?"

Believe it or not, many—maybe even most—of those presented with this opportunity would say, "No." Why? Change is difficult, and habits, even habits like watching television every evening, feel familiar and are difficult to break.

Yet when successful Network Marketers, as entrepreneurs, begin their business, they accept an offer much like this one—whether they know it or not. They choose to take some of their free time and invest it in their future. They make a commitment to study with those more experienced in their field in order to increase their skills, and they put what they learn to immediate use in their business.

Students enrolled in a graduate-level course on Network Marketing would learn to master the basics of the business... They would learn how and where to find prospects, how to present the business to others, and how to teach new distributors so that they can succeed too.

Let's listen in. First, the basics.

There is only one sure-fire way to build a solid Network Marketing business. It requires no selling, no persuasion, and anyone can do it... There are other techniques that require a little more skill—they're next—but the basics will take you anywhere you want to go:

USE YOUR COMPANY'S PRODUCTS AND SERVICES

Whatever your company makes that you can use, use it. If it's a product, don't wait until you run out of what you have on hand. Using all your company's products sets a good example for those who may join you in the business. You never know when the practice may lead to new business.

Imagine one Networker's embarrassment when a friend asked her what nutritional line she was using. If she had been using her company's, she might have won herself a new customer.

EACH MONTH, BUY PRODUCTS TO REMAIN ACTIVE

Buy it, as we say in Network Marketing, "to use, to share, and to sell." Use your company's products or services at home, share them with those you know, and have enough inventory to demonstrate your products to prospective customers as well as those you sponsor.

INITIALLY FIND FOUR PEOPLE

Follow the system... Then help your people find and teach *their* people by following the system too.

That's it.

As you establish your business, your sponsorship line will teach you how to most effectively put the fundamentals of the system into practice, as well as the skills you will need to learn in order to succeed in the most efficient way.

Those are the basic techniques. Now let's look at a few additional ideas for launching a vibrant business:

TELL YOUR FRIENDS, FAMILY, AND CO-WORKERS

Network Marketing is not about reinventing the wheel; it's about following the system. Ask your sponsor how to best share your new business—product, service, and opportunity—with those you know...and be willing to follow their advice.

LIST EVERYONE YOU KNOW

Research shows that everyone knows several hundred people. Therefore, get their names down on paper. You don't need to call them all now, just write down as many names as you can—your next door neighbor, your hairstylist, your sister's best friend. As names come to you, whether first thing in the morning or during dinner or while you're watching a movie, jot them down and add them to your list. Your goal is to make a list of everyone you know by name and then to add to the list as you meet new people.

Review the list often and think about how what you are offering could be of value to the friends you find there. Does someone want to look younger? Perhaps your company offers an effective anti-aging skincare line. Is another friend on the list interested in better health? Perhaps your nutritional supplements would be a good place to start. Has a co-worker mentioned he would like to lose a few pounds? Perhaps your weight loss system would help him regain the body he once had...

Perhaps someone on the list is worried about not having enough money or is concerned about losing contact with their teens. A Network Marketing business can make a terrific family project, especially when everyone knows the additional income will go toward a joint family goal.

DON'T PREJUDGE

Even millionaires may be looking for an opportunity that offers a growing income with less effort or stress. Doctors' incomes, as we mentioned earlier, rely solely on their time with patients, and they tend to have to work long stressful hours to pay for their costs of doing business. Many would welcome a part-time business that allowed them to multiply their efforts by combining them with others. Stockbrokers, bankers, lawyers, captains of industry—all have built successful Networking businesses. In fact, those who are successful in one field often are more able to envision success in another. In other words, don't rule out someone simply because you already see them as successful.

Furthermore, don't be too quick to rule out those who are still struggling to find their place in life. Just as many people who are unemployed, undereducated, or simply underappreciated have risen to find great success in Network Marketing.

PUT YOUR SPONSORSHIP LINE TO WORK

If you decide you would like to grow your business, the best way to do that as a beginner is to find people for your sponsorship line to talk to... Tell people you know about your new venture, and then schedule an appointment to speak with your sponsor with anyone who asks to learn more about your products or about the business opportunity.

"You're right, Alex. I am excited. This is a great company. The products are terrific. And the potential is there for a significant income. But I'm new at this. I'm still learning the ropes myself...

"Tell you what, I'm meeting a business associate at Starbucks on Wednesday. Why don't you join us? I'll probably have only a half-an-hour with her, and I'm sure she'll be able to answer those questions you have about the business."

PUT THE PRINTED WORD TO WORK FOR YOU

Send a press release announcing the opening of your business to your local newspaper. Remember to also inform any specialty business publications in your area.

Pass out your business cards. Go through them as fast as you can... Leave them with your tip at a restaurant. Include them anytime you pay a bill. Be creative!

Some Networkers place advertisements in newspapers and trade journals, looking for others who may want to join them in their business. A Special Report entitled, *Seven Prospecting Secrets* also offers some great tips on where to find the best people for your business. You can receive a free copy by e-mailing your request to: secrets@nexera.com.

PRACTICE A COUPLE OF EASY ICEBREAKERS

Icebreakers allow you to meet people and give you a natural way to talk about your business. For instance, think of how many times you have waited in line at the bank, at the coffee shop, or to buy a ticket for a movie. Perhaps it is your habit to strike up a conversation with the person in front of you and chat for a moment about the weather or current events.

During a natural pause in the conversation, it's very easy to pull out your business card, smile warmly and say:

"You're an easy person to talk with. May I give you my card? You know, I'm always looking for people just like you to work with me in my business. I have no idea if you would be interested in what we're doing, but if you keep your career options open, I would be happy to discuss this with you in more detail. Please, feel free to give me a call anytime."

Then change the subject. You don't need to mention it again. If they're interested or curious, they'll ask you more, and as you gain experience you will become comfortable talking about your business.

USE AUDIO AND VIDEO INFORMATION KITS

One of the most exciting developments in Networking has taken place in just the last few years with the development of content rich CDs and DVDs that tell about Network Marketing or present a company, its products or services, and its business opportunity. The use of these "information kits" can quickly and dramatically multiply your own business-building efforts.

Information kits do two things: They move products and they sponsor distributors. In fact a study by the Wharton School of Business showed that video brochures expedited buying decisions by as much as 72 percent, when compared to print advertising. The study also found that three times as many people were likely to request a DVD as ask for printed information. And they were six times more likely to respond to an offer made in a video brochure than to a printed ad.

Audio and video information kits can be used both locally and long distance as a screening tool. They can help you find those who want to know more about your products or business. Time is money, and information kits are one way to leverage both.

Typically, a Networker builds a number of different kits. Each may contain a CD that tells about the benefits of Network Marketing. It might also include an interesting, easy-to-read book (such as *Future Choice*) that explains how Network Marketing works, or perhaps a short DVD. Networkers simply loan the information kit to someone they know, then return in a day or two to pick it up and answer any questions their friend may have.

Again, let's look at this technique through the doubling concept.

If, as your business grows, you have 10 distributors, each with 10 information kits, that means that at any given time there is the potential for 100 presentations being made. One hundred distributors with 10 kits means the potential for 1,000 presentations, each given exactly the same way.

Do you see how this approach allows you to leverage your effort many times over?

Even if you decide to take a day off, you will know that your representatives, through information kits, are giving professional presentations to hundreds of potential business builders or customers. CDs, DVDs and books are particularly effective because they never have a bad day. They tell the story exactly the same way, every time. They present a true ability to duplicate your message with those you contact and they allow you to quickly reach many people.

If you choose to rapidly build your business, experienced Networkers recommend that you pass out at least two information kits, three days a week. Two days after you loan out the first kits, return to pick them up. Answer any questions, and then pass them on to someone else. Two days later, pick up those kits and do the same thing... You will be contacting 12 people a week—those you gave the kits to last week and those they're going to this week.

One comfortable way to pass out information kits about your company (or actual product for prospects to try) is called a third-party referral system: You simply ask those you know to refer you to someone else who might be interested in what your company has to offer. When you talk with that person, mention who made the referral. If you were to make contact by telephone, the conversation could go like this:

> *"Jan, my name is John Smith. Sandy Nelson and I were visiting yesterday and she suggested I give you a call. My wife and I have just started a new business and we're looking for a few sharp people to work with us. Sandy spoke very highly of you and mentioned you might be exactly what we're looking for. I'm curious, are you open to any offers?"*

Jan is sure to want to know more! Even if it turns out that she is not interested, she may know someone who is. A variation to the third-party referral offers the chance to obtain even more contacts.

> *"Jan, my name is John Smith. Sandy Nelson suggested that I give you a call. My wife and I have just started a new business and Sandy thought you might know of someone who is looking for a substantial part-time income. Jan, who do you know that might be interested in earning an extra $500 to $2,000 per month?"*

AVOID A HARD-SELL APPROACH

Each of our suggested business-builder ideas relies on an easy and natural way of talking with people. That's important. Because contrary to popular belief, Network Marketing is not about selling products to strangers...

Today consumers and potential distributors are more sophisticated. No one wants to be browbeaten, even with the financial opportunity of a lifetime. Sharp Networkers inform people of what they're doing, let them know they would like to do business with them and then keep in touch, lightly. They look for ways to offer value and they let people know they respect their ability to make decisions that are right for them at any given time.

The only additional key to any successful Network Marketing venture is to learn what works and repeat it. Repeat it again, then teach those you sponsor to repeat it. It's a concept known in the business as, "following the system." Because systems create results—duplicatable results.

It's true. All efforts in Networking are measured by whether they can be easily and correctly duplicated. As author and noted success trainer Anthony Robbins teaches, "Success leaves clues." Therefore, to achieve the level of success you desire, just follow the clues...

You don't have to figure out Network Marketing on your own. You can select a company that already is enjoying a high level of success. And you can choose with whom to work from any number of talented people in your successline. It's not like going to work for IBM. In the traditional corporate world, you can't decide which company you want to represent, and then walk in, find out who is the nicest boss and request to work only with them.

But you can in Network Marketing. After you have been sponsored, you can "go upline" and speak to your sponsor's sponsor, and to their sponsor, and to their sponsor, until you find the person that you feel comfortable with. You can usually talk with these leaders and many times even request one of them to be your personal mentor. If they are the type of leader you are looking for, they will be pleased to work with you.

In addition to working personally with your own mentor, each successline contains top leaders who through conference calls, e-mail blasts, and live events, can offer you many valuable insights. And leaders in the Network Marketing industry itself have authored many excellent guides to success. You can find some favorites listed in the back of this book. Indeed, your company's training systems, combined with those provided and recommended by your successline, will quickly get you started on your advanced degree. With them, you will have proven methods for success available to you from the first minute you open your business.

Michael S. Clouse

7.

CHALLENGES AND CHOICES

"All truth passes through three stages.
First, it is ridiculed.
Second, it is violently opposed.
Third, it is accepted as being self-evident."
—Author Schopenhauer
German philosopher (1788 - 1860)

I T'S GOING TO HAPPEN, so you might as well plan for it. It could be your sister, your mother, or your best friend, your co-worker, or your golfing buddy brimming with excitement. You're going ask someone whose opinion you value about your new business. And before you're even halfway finished describing it, they will look at you and say, with the same tone of voice they use to discuss the Internal Revenue Service, "This sounds like one of those illegal pyramid schemes."

And then their mind will snap shut. You'll hear it clang closed; nothing you can say will make a difference. It happens to everyone...

Some people just don't want to hear about Network Marketing. Ever! Even if they love you and would ordinarily support you in any way they could. Some people are just suspicious of the unfamiliar. Or maybe they've been hit by one too many hard-sells. Maybe they know someone who had a bad experience in the industry. Perhaps they themselves at one time chose a bad company or suffered through a bad sponsor. Either way, they may have ended up with a garage full of products, a credit card full of charges, or an address book full of former friends.

Ouch!

Luckily, if you choose to become involved in Network Marketing, most of those you approach with your new venture will be delighted at your enthusiasm and open to what you have to present. But if you find yourself hurt when someone you care about doesn't seem happy for you, take a deep breath and then take a second look at their reaction.

They may be leery that you're going to pester them to buy things they don't want or ask them repeatedly to join a company they don't care about.

Even success can be threatening; they may fear you will change and grow away from them. They may even assume everyone else shares their opinion about Network Marketing and urge you to drop the idea. All of those things are okay.

Over time, they'll see that, although you talk about your company with enthusiasm, you let them decide at what level they want to be involved. They will discover that your business adds to your life. It doesn't take you away from theirs.

"I made it a point early on that my close friends and family would have to *ask* me about my business," says one seasoned Networker. "And now they do."

Sooner or later, those who were skeptical *will* ask to try a product or two and before you know it, some of those family members will become your biggest fans.

Until then, believe it or not, not everyone needs to share your enthusiasm for your business. Although it would be ideal to have the wholehearted support of your spouse, your family and your friends from the beginning, it's not required. The reality is many Networking fortunes have been built over others' objections, yet by the time those fortunes were well under way, most doubters had long before climbed on board.

Not everyone will want to try your products, and not everyone will want to join your company. But plenty will. Your job is to find the ones who will.

How?

By sorting.

Perhaps one of the oldest Network Marketing stereotypes is that Networkers try to trick people into doing business with them or that they berate friends and family into buying their products.

How unproductive and unprofessional.

Today's Networkers stress the word Networking. They seek to build long-term business relationships based on respect and integrity. They do business with associates in a way that is mutually beneficial by offering valuable goods and services to a growing and willing marketplace. As they prosper, they are able to offer their business opportunity as an exciting possibility for others. Perhaps more than anything else, they demonstrate that Networking is convenient and pleasant.

To find their markets, good Networkers "sort" through people.

They speak honestly about their company, their products and their business. When appropriate, they offer to share their information and enthusiasm with others. They never try to convince anyone, and they don't take rejection personally.

"You never know why someone says 'No,'" says one experienced business-builder. "Maybe it's not the right time for them. Maybe they're feeling overwhelmed. Maybe they've had a bad day. Just remember, a 'No' doesn't necessarily mean no. It can mean, 'maybe later.'

"Rejections happen to all of us. If you're not getting rejections, you're not working your business. When it happens to me, I just make a note of the conversation and move on. Because they're really not saying 'No' to me, they're saying 'No' to this opportunity right now."

One Seattle Networker agrees, with a witty twist.

His designer auto license plates read, "SWSWSW." When asked what the letters meant, he said, "I'm looking for people who are looking. I sort for a living. And every time I approach my car, my license plates remind me of my personal philosophy. The letters stand for, 'Some Will, Some Won't, So What!'"

Indeed!

As Network Marketers build their businesses, some will choose to join. Others won't. So what!

Modern Network Marketing can offer new business-builders the training and education they need to make their businesses a success. It also can offer advice that will help newcomers avoid the disappointment and defeat that pioneers in Network Marketing experienced. In general, inexperienced Network Marketers make one common mistake...

Nine out of 10 people who feel they have failed at Network Marketing believe the company, the product, or the concept just doesn't work. They hear about the industry's superstars, the ones who ended their first year in the business with a $100,000 income and a white Mercedes-Benz in the garage. Then after only a few weeks or months, when they don't see the same results in their own business, they get discouraged and quit.

Hear this, now!

There are only three basic elements to success in Network Marketing: choosing the right company for you, following the system, and continuing *until* you achieve success. By contrast, those who fail do so for only one reason—they quit too soon, assuming they chose the right company, and followed the system.

When that happens, success doesn't bypass their group. It just bypasses them.

Think for a moment about a new doctor, setting up a first practice. Would that doctor consider the beginning of his or her business to be the day he or she first entered medical school, or rather from the day he or she accepted the first patient? Is there any doubt he or she would consider the beginning of the business to be from the day they actually began to practice medicine, *after* completion of their education?

Yet new Networkers too often start counting how long they have been in business from the day they sign on with a company, even if they have no prior experience in Network Marketing. They are too hard on themselves; they allow no time for education. Then, if their new business doesn't yield a significant profit immediately, they get discouraged. They end up looking for the rewards of an advanced degree when they're only halfway through the undergraduate program.

Remember our fictitious friends, Andy and Samantha? At the end of their first year in Networking, they had few distributors, little sales volume, and no business-builders in sight. But they continued their work...

One year later, they were working with Samantha's Uncle Mike and a growing group in Detroit. Before long, they had been joined by Andy's sister's friend, Janet, who quickly developed her own group. Within three years, their struggling little venture had evolved into a prosperous and growing business enterprise.

Tom Schreiter, a top national Networker known for his series of "Big Al" training books, tells a similar story.

Tom and his wife became Networkers when Tom was in his early 20s. Without the training tools available to Networkers today, they managed to make about every mistake possible. After almost two years, they had no distributors, no sales volume and few prospects for the future. But that didn't stop them.

"We didn't know we could quit," Tom says, laughing at his own story. "Our sponsor didn't tell us we had that option." He and his wife continued to work at their business and today Tom Schreiter is one of Networking's superstars. He has reached his goals and fulfilled his dreams, simply because he did not give up.

As a beginning Network Marketer, you will do a lot of things that you don't immediately get paid for. But as your business grows, there will come a day when you will be paid for a lot of things you no longer do. That's what makes Network Marketing different from working for someone else. When you have a job, you exchange your time for your employer's money. In Network Marketing, you exchange time up front for a substantial income later.

8.

SUCCESS DOES LEAVE CLUES

"Go confidently in the direction of your dreams!
Live the life you've imagined."
—Henry David Thoreau

MEET DANA COLLINS, CECILIA STOLL, DEANA WILKINSON, AND TOM "BIG AL" SCHREITER. All of these entrepreneurs have built large, successful Network Marketing businesses, but they may best be known for how skillfully they pass along to others what they have learned. Their commitment is to teach others how to achieve as they have. If success does leave clues, these four certainly have many of the answers.

Dana Collins knows all to well that on most mornings women across the country get up before sunrise, wake sleeping children, and put on panty hose—then rush sleepy-eyed children off to daycare, or school—so they can spend their early morning hours fighting traffic, hoping to get to work on time.

However, because of the success of their home-based business, mornings around the Collins' house are a bit more relaxed these days. "Scott and I are just waking up at 8:00 am, and only because we need to get our older children, Jack and Grace, ready to catch the school bus at 9:00 am." After breakfast together as a family, backpacks are donned and the Collins clan, dog included, walk to the bus stop to see their children off before officially beginning their day...

But just a few short years ago things were very different. Dana and her husband, Scott, had just moved from Seattle to the east coast. They left behind their jobs and financed the move themselves. That decision created enormous debt. "I remember being unemployed for six months," Dana said. "And the day I finally received a substantial job offer, I was introduced to Network Marketing.

When Dana told her mom about the incredible job offer she had received her mother asked her what turned out to be, quite literally, the mega-million dollar question: "If you take that position," her mom queried, "where will you be in five years?"

Having been both a business owner and corporate employee before, and wanting to have more choices and flexibility in her life than the demanding position being offered might allow, Dana considered her options...

"I remembered that as a self-employed person, I had created my own job. But in order to make more money, I had to work more hours too. And there simply hadn't been enough hours in the week to be the boss *and* have a life."

Dana had thought a corporate position was the answer, but found she had little control over her time or income. Vacations were limited to two weeks a year and unless she could somehow become the CEO, there was an income ceiling.

Evaluating her options and the question posed to her by her mom, "If you take this position, where will you be in five years?" Dana made what some might consider a radical career move. She chose Network Marketing.

"I felt as if someone had finally shared with me the secret to earning a living *and* having a life." Dana recalls, "In business school we learned that ownership is a key to wealth. But most of us can't afford ownership, nor do we want the headaches that come with owning a business and having employees. We are also taught that leveraging other peoples time, or leveraging other peoples money are the keys to our success, but we aren't taught how. When I learned about the brilliant business model of Network Marketing, I thought, this is the missing piece of the puzzle. I'm in!"

For the first few of years in her business, Dana earned a few thousand dollars a month—enough to make a difference in her family's lifestyle. However, things in her husband's world were getting difficult.

Working in medical sales, Scott had sold so much in his territory the company asked him to work in another state so they could catch up with the sales he had generated. This required Scott to be away from home five days a week. To add insult to injury, Scott's boss was very unsympathetic about Scott having a toddler at home and a wife with another child on the way.

"I realized then that Scott was working for the evil empire and needed to be rescued," Dana said. "So I decided to give my business my all for one year so Scott would have more options." At the end of that year Scott was able to make a career move of his own and pursue his dream. "Because that year was so successful, we thought, what if I kept going for another year?" Four years later, Dana and her team had built a small empire. As an Independent Executive National Vice President with her company, Dana's total business revenue is approaching $100,000,000 a year!

Dana's goals have grown, along with her achievements. Not only has she been able to gain time and financial freedom for her and her family, she has also helped hundreds of other consultants in her successline and thousands within other organizations as well. The tangible measure of her efforts show up in many ways, one of the most visible being nearly 100 people in her organization alone are now driving a white Mercedes-Benz, the car consultants qualify to receive after reaching the Independent Regional Vice President status with her company.

"While Network Marketing presents an amazing opportunity to develop an income stream most people only dream of, it is the *lifestyle opportunity* that is truly remarkable," Dana said. "The benefits of time leveraging and developing an ongoing income stream can provide a buffer from the roadblocks life can throw in front of you in the form of financial hardship, illness, or family needs.

The one message Dana Collins would love everyone to know is this: "While Network Marketing isn't for *everyone*; it can be a great opportunity for *anyone*. I'm not an extraordinary person, I just live an extraordinary life, and so can you."

Cecilia Stoll began her Network Marketing journey in 1991 because she wanted to purchase her products at wholesale and offer them to a few friends. Becoming an Independent National Vice President—the top position in her company—didn't even cross her mind. "I knew I was an ordinary person," Cecilia said, "and I thought great things only happened to extraordinary people."

Working as a secretary—the only job in Edmond, Oklahoma she could get with her psychology degree—Cecilia was frustrated with the "8 to 5" routine and the paycheck-to-paycheck mentality that had already become a part of life. "My husband and I didn't have any money for vacations or extra things," Cecilia said. "When I envisioned my life five years down the road, things looked bleak."

The Stolls knew when they started their family that they wanted Cecilia to be home with the children. But becoming a single-income family would make matters even worse. "I knew if I kept doing what I was doing, I would continue to get what I'd got. I had to do something different."

That something different turned out to be Network Marketing... "My dear friend, Martha McIntyre, brought me a skincare sample pack to try. I loved the products and became a consultant. Martha helped me with my first three presentations and then I was on my own," Cecilia said. "I remember getting ready for my first solo presentation. I was scared to death! I was hyperventilating, my voice was shaking, I had red blotches on my neck—I read what I had prepared word-for-word because I was too nervous to remember anything! I was a mess... However, people bought products that night, and I had a major revelation: Speaking in front of a group didn't kill me!"

Cecilia knew that night she could make some extra money and maybe even replace her income. "Six months after joining my company, I jumped in with both feet," Cecilia said. "I earned my white Mercedes-Benz cash bonus three years after joining the company. Three years after that—and just five days before giving birth to our second child—I became an Independent National Vice President."

Although it was not always a smooth ride, Cecilia and her family believed it was worth the sacrifice! "I struggled with everything everyone else struggles with building the business: rejection, cancellations, no shows, people's lack of belief in me and the opportunity, time away from home, late nights, early mornings... For some time I was the only person on my team committed enough to go to the meetings, Cecilia said. "I was a team of one, but I did not give myself the option to quit."

The lessons Cecilia learned along the way are many... "I learned this business can be worked part-time, but not sometimes. I learned if you're not 'coachable' you won't be a great coach. I learned there are no shortcuts. I learned going to meetings and company conferences are not optional. I learned in the beginning if you spend money to build your business, there will come a day when, with one check, you can pay off all your bills and have plenty left over! I learned your commitment is directly reflected on your calendar. I learned courage is not the absence of fear; it is the willingness to do what needs to be done. I learned you can't pass on belief to people who are not willing to receive it. I learned your checks grow when you grow. Finally, I learned even though the mountain you're climbing is high, and sometimes rocky, the view from the top is breathtaking!"

The life and lifestyle that Cecilia, her husband Marvin, and their children have achieved is almost impossible to imagine... "Besides being debt-free, we get to choose any doctor we need, regardless of whether or not he or she is on our insurance plan. Our children are able to attend a private Christian school. My husband, Marvin, was able to turn down a job transfer, even though it meant the loss of his job—because he no longer needed to work. We can, and do, go on mission trips to foreign countries *and* we are able to assist other families financially who wouldn't otherwise be able to go. Best of all—because of the financial success this business has afforded our family—my mom, who lives in Brazil, can now come and visit her grandchildren anytime she wants."

The friendships, and personal growth are but two of the many benefits this journey has given Cecilia Stoll. "I am hardly the person I was back in 1991. And if it all ended tomorrow, I know today I am a better wife, mom, and friend because of what I learned as a result of this business." A deeply religious person, Cecilia's story wouldn't be complete without respectfully acknowledging her Creator... "I thank the Lord for being my strength, my guide, and the only One worthy of all glory and praise, without whom I would be nothing!"

Deana Wilkinson had already tried her hand at direct sales, without much success, before she was introduced to her company in 1988. "I had only sponsored three people in my former business," Deana said. "I really wanted to make an extra $500 a month. Finally, I was able to accomplish that, so life was great...or so I thought."

Unfortunately, Deana's husband's business had experienced a sudden downturn and she was feeling pressured at home to get back into corporate America.

"I couldn't stomach the thought of putting on panty hose and fighting traffic at 6 o'clock in the morning," Deana said. "I had been a stay-at-home mom for 13 years and things needed to remain that way because our oldest son, Ben, was born with Cerebral Palsy... I fought hard for him as the first child with a disability to be mainstreamed at his school and I knew if I went back to work they would return him to a special education class."

About that time Donna Johnson came to Salt Lake City, Utah, and Deana was invited to join her, along with seven other women, for lunch. When they first met, Donna was a single mother of three and had been in Arbonne for only 17 months—just five months longer than Deana. "I remember sitting next to Donna and then at one point she left the table for a moment. I couldn't help but notice her organizer was open and her last Arbonne paycheck was tucked inside. I resisted the temptation for about one second and then I leaned over and peeked at her check. When I saw the amount, it was as if the skies were opened and I could see a way out of our financial problems. I realized then, if I treated this like a *real* business, I could create an income that would allow me to be home with our three sons."

That evening, Deana told her husband about her experience and her plan. "He looked at me like I was insane and said, 'How are *you* going to become a Manager? You can't sponsor anyone!' But those words didn't stop her. "When someone questions your dream, you can buy into their belief, or you can buy into your own.

I chose the 'I'll show you!' plan," Deana said.

Within five months Deana had 180 people on her rapidly-growing team. "My husband realized then what an incredible opportunity we had and became supportive very quickly," Deana said. For the first time Deana and her husband Richard started to believe they could do more than just financially survive. "We only had one car at that time," Deana said. "Every time I needed to go somewhere I had to ask someone for a ride. Just the thought of getting another car, let alone a white Mercedes-Benz, got us both excited."

Because of the car program offered by her company, Deana and Richard went to the Mercedes-Benz dealership, picked up some brochures, cut out pictures of the car they wanted, and then put them all over their house! "I knew we had gone over the edge when I lifted the toilet seat and there was a photo of the car we wanted taped under the lid. But a little more than a year later, I was driving a white Mercedes-Benz!

Deana learned from watching *South Pacific*, you've got to have a dream—a dream so grand it might be impossible to achieve! Today, of course, their dream has been accomplished... "My Network Marketing career has blessed our family in so many ways," Deana said. "If someone had tried to describe to me five years ago what our life would be like right now, I wouldn't have believed them..."

This year the Wilkinson's home-based business will surpass $100,000,000 in annual sales—and it continues to grow—providing the family with a comfortable seven figure annual income.

As a family, the Wilkinson's have traveled the world many times on company trips, and their children have been able to study abroad—gaining a well-rounded education. Richard was able to retire in the spring of 2003 from a stressful business that owned him for 26 years, and now Deana and Richard work together. Indeed, Deana and Richard agree, their partnership has greatly enriched both their business and their married life.

Tom Schreiter was born on a Nebraska farm. He joined his first Network Marketing Company early, in 1972 at age 23. "I got married," he said. "And like most married couples, we needed extra money. I could either work a part-time job until I was 65 to make ends meet, or I could have a part-time business in Network Marketing. It was the only business I could afford. Back then, it cost $18.75 to get started—and we financed that."

Tom saw an ad in the newspaper, went to an opportunity meeting, and liked what he saw.

"For the first eighteen months, my wife and I were probably the hardest working couple you ever saw," he said. "We went to every opportunity meeting, every training meeting, and every company function. We made a lot of retail presentations and yet at the end of eighteen months, we basically had no customers and no distributors. So, the first eighteen months were a little bit slow..."

Yet they never thought of quitting.

"We didn't know we could quit," Tom said. "We didn't have any downline to quit. We didn't have any customers to quit. And our sponsor never told us we could quit. So we didn't know it was possible. We just assumed that was it. Hooked forever! But being naive paid off. After eighteen months, we got our first break."

Almost two years after they had started their business, the Schreiters sponsored their first business-builder. "That got us some customers and a little momentum," Tom said.

The slow start didn't discourage them. Because the Schreiters had made the decision their first night that Network Marketing was to be their future.

"Our major problem was, we had no skills, or any idea how to do this," he said. "Back then, there was nobody to provide training. No books, no general training courses." Instead, we learned the old-fashioned way, with plenty of trials and more than a few errors.

Today, Tom bases his training on practical, easy-to-duplicate principles that provide a clear picture of what Network Marketing has to offer. He presents it all with a grin and with a realistic idea of what it will take to make it to the top.

And he doesn't promise quick or easy riches.

"What I think works best is to talk with a person who is already making $5,000 a month and who would like to make $1,500 a month part-time on top of that," he said. "Because in that $5,000 budget, after paying all the bills, a person may only have $150 left over. By adding $1,500 a month, you've taken that amount 10 times further."

The additional income can make the difference between financial discomfort and prosperity. "You could throw that $1,500 into the bank, and with interest, become a millionaire in 20 years," Tom said. "Or you could take a nice vacation for two to Cancun several times a year. There are so many things you can do with an extra $1,500 a month. A regular job takes care of all your needs, and this is *extra* money!"

Tom looks for people who are willing to invest effort into their business and into themselves. "The secret to long-term success in Network Marketing is to create leaders by teaching them how to become successful," he said. "I look for people who want to become leaders. They may not have the skills yet, but that's okay, if they're willing, they can learn."

That's when "Big Al" begins his education process.

Tom's advice: "Scratch out the first six months to learn the business, become your own best customer, and then, as you begin to understand the business, teach others."

At the end of six months, those who make a solid commitment to Network Marketing should be able to make a good presentation, and should also be working with several potential leaders of their own, Tom said. At the end of their first year, they could have "a couple of very good leaders and $5,000 to $7,000 a month in extra income," as well as a good start on a secure future.

As he talks with people, Tom looks for those who are open to Network Marketing.

"I look for prospects who *want* the benefits this business offers, rather than trying to persuade them they *need* the benefits," he said. "While the inexperienced Networker spends their time trying to convince someone, I look for those who don't need convincing."

So far, Tom's series of "Big Al" books have taught the basics of Network Marketing to over 20 million of today's Networkers throughout the world.

"We wrote the first book because we made all these mistakes," he said in the voice of Big Al's straight man. "Then we made some more mistakes and wrote the second one. We made some more mistakes and wrote the third one; made a *lot* of mistakes and wrote the fourth and fifth ones. All we really do is list our mistakes so people can say, 'Yeah, I did that too,' or maybe, 'I can avoid that one.'"

According to Tom "Big Al" Schreiter, "Network Marketing is about sponsoring people who *want* to become successful, and then teaching them *how* to become leaders. It's making a long-term investment in people. It's not 'get-rich-quick,' and yet for those who learn the business and then stay the course, there is an opportunity to do quite well."

9.

A Beginning

"The future belongs to those who believe
in the beauty of their dreams."
—Eleanor Roosevelt

*T*he children ran ahead as Tom and Susan Edison
stepped off their jetway and began to climb the
brick path toward their house. It was good to
be home.

*One of the best parts of their business was the chance
it gave them to travel the world, visiting associates who
long ago had become friends. But another was the opportunity to return, as always, here to their home. After
a couple of weeks away, a huge glass house nestled in a
meadow alongside a high Colorado lake seemed just the
place to be.*

*"Andy and Samantha looked good, didn't they?" Su-
san asked Tom, unconsciously reaching out for his hand*

113

as they walked. "I think she's right. Her new group is going to take off. Looks like the next few months will be busy ones for her—and for me."

"You've taught her well," Tom said. "And the leaders she's attracting are sharp. You'll probably be able to handle most of your end from here, don't you think?"

"Yes. I don't plan to stir for the entire winter. There are too many things I want to do here. Like gaze into a fire."

Tom laughed. "I've heard that before," he said. "Remember what you used to say when you were first starting the business? 'I can inch my way to the top where I am or I can fly to the top on my own.' You've really taken flight, Sue."

Susan squeezed his hand and laughed. "You thought I was crazy," she said. "It took you two years to admit I hadn't taken leave of every single one of my senses. Remember my first bonus check? Not quite $28."

She paused. "Where do you suppose we would have ended up if we hadn't become Networkers?" she asked.

"Wherever it would have been, it would have been okay," Tom said, as they reached their deck. "We would have made sure of that. I'm just glad we made the choices we did when we did. Come on, do you want to download a movie, or screen the new product holograms? David said he'd have them here this evening."

"You go ahead," Susan said, sinking into a chair beside the pool. "I'm going to sit here for a few minutes and watch the sun set."

Dusk gathered as Susan leaned back in her chair

and thought back to their trip and to the friends they had visited. Tomorrow would be a busy day...

As the meadow darkened, the lights inside the house began to cast brighter reflections into the hydropool until they seemed to pull her inside to her family.

"Look back?" she said to herself as she got up and turned to the house. "No. Not ever."

The distance between ourselves and our futuristic friend, Susan Edison, may not be that great. Networking companies are already using an amazing array of technology to revolutionize the way they communicate with representatives and with those who want to learn more about their company and their products.

One example is Arbonne International. Founded in 1980, and today one of the fastest growing Network Marketing companies in the world, Arbonne continues to find innovative ways to teach, update, and inspire its 800,000+ customers, wholesale buyers, and business-builders alike.

For business-builders, Arbonne University is available online anytime, providing lessons from basic consultant training, to product knowledge, to managing and leading an ever-growing organization. And that's not all... ArbonneMultimedia, also available 24/7, allows *anyone* to view information on new product releases and convention promotions online, or to simply download the video to a computer or iPod for later viewing.

In addition to on-demand education, top leaders

also play a key role in ensuring consultants are properly trained. Arbonne's Learn & Burn™ series, a weekly interview-style program hosted by Arbonne's President, Rita Davenport, offers tips, techniques, and training information that can be downloaded to a computer, burned onto a CD, or transferred to an iPod and then listened to by consultants anywhere in the world.

With a special focus on personal development, Arbonne regularly hosts live events that attract 17 to 17,000 enthusiastic business-builders as well as interested guests. And no one does a better job of recognizing individual achievement than Arbonne... From the hundreds of *Eye on Arbonne* success stories, available on Arbonne.com, to their car program—all Independent Regional Vice Presidents and Independent National Vice Presidents qualify to drive a white Mercedes-Benz—Arbonne has indeed found a way to make their leaders feel important.

And yet, technology aside, it is the *culture* of the Company, driven by Rita Davenport, which is the real reason Arbonne is flourishing... Known throughout the organization as *"The Arbonne Way,"* their approach to business *is* different. For example, top leaders routinely travel to train other teams—because they want to and because they can. "What's working?" ideas that often come from the field are willingly shared with corporate, and then turned into systems *everyone* can use. Throughout the company, "TEAM" is not just an acronym for Together Everyone Achieves More; it is

"The Arbonne Way."

Although the future suggests we embrace these *"Hi-Tech"* advancements, corporate staff, employees, leaders and consultants alike will need to find a way to move forward faster without sacrificing the personal human experience of *"Hi-Touch."* Arbonne understands this and its results serve as self-evident.

Research suggests these high-technology approaches to business, along with the correct company culture, herald the communication and business revolution that lies ahead.

Technology is already cutting new frontiers through the way we live our lives, until it seems our futures are racing toward us at the speed of light. Even though we sometimes feel we are whirling in a confusion of change, we know the decisions we make today will shape all else that is to come.

Like those early in the century who watched with awe the approach of Halley's Comet, we all can choose to view the future with apprehension or with awe and anticipation.

That choice is yours.

When the next decade finds Susan Edison on her Colorado mountaintop, I believe those who today choose Network Marketing also will find themselves looking out over their own vistas of opportunity and accomplishment.

That too is your *Future Choice.*

Michael S. Clouse

POSTSCRIPT

A S YOU MAKE THE CHOICES that shape your future, my thoughts and good wishes go with you. I invite you to learn more about Network Marketing and about how your own home-based business can help you build the life you desire. I've listed a number of excellent resources in the back of this book and how you can obtain them…

And please, feel free to contact me directly as well. If I don't know the answers to your questions, I'll help you find them. After all, that's how Network Marketing works….

All the best,

MSC

Michael S. Clouse
msc@nexera.com

Michael S. Clouse

Appendix A:
Overcome the
No-Time Syndrome

Millions of Network Marketing distributors are building successful part-time businesses in their spare time. And yet perhaps you're thinking, "I'd like to, but I just don't have the time..." There are 168 hours in every single week. Where does the time go? Take a good long look:

Activity	Time Spent		Time remaining in the week
Sleep:	8 hours/day	56 hours/week	112 hours
Full time job:	8 hours/day	40 hours/week	72 hours
Commuting:	2 hours/day	10 hours/week	62 hours
Eating:	2 hours/day	14 hours/week	48 hours
Family & entertainment:	2 hours/day	14 hours/week	34 hours
Miscellaneous:	2 hours/day	14 hours/week	20 hours

So where do the remaining 20 hours typically go?

According to the A.C. Nielsen Co., the average American watches more than four hours of TV each day (or 28 hours per week, or two months of nonstop TV-watching per year). In a 65-year life, that person will have spent nine years glued to the tube! How much is the TV habit costing you? $5,000 a year? $10,000 a year? More? Rethinking your TV habit and investing a few extra hours into your own home-based business could make you rich. In other words, you can either watch *Who Wants To Be A Millionaire*, or you can become one! That, again, is your *Future Choice*.

APPENDIX B:
ETHICS

Seven ways to gauge a company's integrity:

1. Today's quality Network Marketing companies *offer legitimate goods and services at prices consumers are willing to pay.* The company's retail prices should favorably compare to the main-stream marketplace.

2. *Compensation is based on the movement of products, goods, and services—not recruitment.* Distributors earn commissions and bonuses based on the amount of sales volume, either individual or in their group. Income should never be earned for recruiting alone.

3. *Sale of goods and services must be the company's primary focus, not the growth of its distribution network.* Look for a company with a balanced approached to acquiring customers and distributors.

4. You will need inventory. However, *legitimate Network*

Marketing companies don't require distributors to buy inventory to start their businesses. They also have liberal buy-back policies in the event a distributor chooses to leave the business.

5. *Income claims are only allowed when accompanied by a full company disclosure.* Although the rewards can be staggering, those in the company, and its networks, are diligent in fairly representing income potential. Network Marketing is not a get-rich-quick scheme. As with any business venture, it rewards those who consistently follow a proven system for success. Make sure you get the whole income story!

6. Look for a *proven management track record.* Whether a company has been around for years or has just begun, look for a record of successful top management. Some of today's most exciting companies are the product of years of experience by industry leaders who continue to introduce improvements and innovation into Network Marketing.

7. *Company information is easy to obtain and is positive in scope.* The Direct Selling Association (dsa.org), Multi-Level Marketing International Association (mlmia.com), the Federal Trade Commission (ftc.gov), state attorneys general and other consumer groups offer additional information on how to judge Network Marketing and other business opportunities. If you enjoy using the

product or service, become a customer. If you would like to build a business, acquire accurate information, decide if Network Marketing is for you, and then get started on your future!

Michael S. Clouse

BIOGRAPHY

MICHAEL S. CLOUSE HAS AUTHORED NUMEROUS articles, books, and CD programs on the subject of Network Marketing. Certified as a Network Marketing Professional by the University of Illinois at Chicago, Michael is an experienced success coach and a dynamic educational speaker.

Often quoted by best-selling author Richard Poe in *The Wave 3 Way To Building Your Downline*, and Poe's subsequent book, *Wave 4*, Michael's background includes extensive experience in direct sales, motivational psychology and Network Distribution.

An internationally recognized Network Marketing expert, Michael has appeared on business radio shows, as well as the occasional television talk show. His weekly newsletter, Nexera e-News™, is read by tens of thousands of Network Marketing Professionals around the world.

To contact Michael, visit: www.nexera.com/msc.

THE FIFTH PRINCIPLE

"Is The Fifth Principle great
stuff? Try this test: Buy 10. Give
them to your people—even
and especially your business
prospects—and ask each of
them to read it in 24 hours.
(That's easy.) At the end of
your current pay-period,
subtract the costs of the
books from the increase in

your check. Use 10 percent of that amount to buy more
books. Keep doing that for one year. Then do whatever
you desire for the rest of your life."

—John Milton Fogg
Author of *The Greatest Networker in the World*

Your 90 Day Game Plan

Prospecting, presentation, duplication, leadership.

Listen to this step-by-step, connect-the-dots, build-your-business-faster audio program, and you'll learn:

1) how to get your business started right,
2) prospecting, presentation, and duplication, and
3) the secret to finding and developing leaders.

If you want to succeed in your business, listening to—and learning from—this audio training program is an absolute must!

To order yours: visit www.nexera.com/90
U.S.A. 1 888 639 3722 International +1 425 774 4264

Thinking Your Way To Success

"Change your thinking and you will change your life!"

This is the most powerful information on the mind I have ever assembled... It explains why only a few distributors succeed, *and* why far too many simply fail—and how you can use your mind to become one of the top performers in your company, build a great business, and truly live an extraordinary life! Get these CDs into the hands of every distributor you have on you team—and experience the power of *"Knowledge Applied!"*

This program contains three CDs, the complete PowerPoint outline, and includes, *"The 38 Philosophies"* bonus CD by Michael S. Clouse.

To order yours: visit www.nexera.com/think
U.S.A. 1 888 639 3722 International +1 425 774 4264

Your Prospecting Toolbox

"Learn where to find two new prospects every day—in any city you choose!"

To order yours: visit
www.nexera.com/ypt
U.S.A.   1 888 639 3722
International +1 425 774 4264

The Simple Art of Duplication

"What you need to know to build a business that duplicates!"

This program contains one CD, and features an interview with Art Jonak and Michael S. Clouse.

To order yours: visit www.nexera.com/art
U.S.A.   1 888 639 3722   International +1 425 774 4264

Your Total Success Pack

Your Total Success Pack comes with seven of our best-selling audio programs, 19 CDs, the complete set of downloadable e-Books, and step-by-step instructions for each program!

These audio programs will teach you exactly how to create *Total Success* in your business and in your life! If you're ready to build a better future, order yours now!

To order yours: visit www.nexera.com/tsp
U.S.A. 1 888 639 3722 International +1 425 774 4264

REQUEST MICHAEL S. CLOUSE LIVE

If you coordinate your team's live training events and would like to request Michael S. Clouse as your guest speaker, simply e-mail the dates and details to info@nexera.com

RECIPE FOR SUCCESS

Apply the simple, effective, and time-tested techniques revealed on this 75 minute training CD, and you will be able to easily go from the bottom 5% of the distributors in your company, to the top 5% of the distributors in your company, in less than five years!

To order yours: visit www.nexera.com/rfs
U.S.A. 1 888 639 3722 International +1 425 774 4264

BUILDING A BETTER LIFE

What would it take for you to really have it all?

Imagine a life—your life—filled with a loving family and close friends. Imagine earning an income beyond your wildest dreams.

Imagine having the free time to travel the world, to volunteer for a worthy cause, or to simply do whatever you please...

Does this sound too good to be true? Well, what if it were possible? Would you be willing to learn—and then try—a few simple strategies that could allow you to truly build a better life?

This 8 CD program, recorded live, will teach you the exact steps to take—what to focus on and what to skip—to create balance in your business and live the life of your dreams. Order yours now!